# All the Stuff You Need to Know About RVing

Dr. Ronald E. Jones

Robert G. Lowe

RonJon Publishing, Inc.

*Cover Design*
>  Jerry D. Boyle Jr.

© 2004   RonJon Publishing, Inc.


ISBN 1-56870-514-X

First Edition

Printed in the United States of America

For information, contact:

RonJon Publishing, Inc.
1001 S. Mayhill Rd.
Denton, Texas 76208
(940) 383-3060
Information@ronjonpublishing.com

Library of Congress Control Number:  2004094101


1 2 3 4 5 6 7 8 9 10   BPMN   05

This book is dedicated to our life's traveling partners—
Sandy and Jane—together with our families.

# *Table of Contents*

# *Foreword*

Traveling by Recreational Vehicle—RVing—is one of the most rewarding ways to explore this great planet. You see places often just read about, you meet people that quickly become friends, and you travel in safety and comfort. Modern RVs are certainly more than a mode of travel—they have become a lifestyle.

Whether you want to start exploring together as a family or your family has grown and moved in various directions, you can visit all of them and explore in an RV. You sleep in your own bed, have meals as you would at home, and enjoy all the creature comforts of home. In fact, many RVers enjoy more comforts in their RV than they have at home. You can become a modern day "gypsy" with your home being where you are staying today. As one RVer always replies when asked where she lives, "Right over there."

There are two authors and we asked spouses, friends, sales reps, campground owners, and many other RVers for their suggestions. We often ended up with several ways to accomplish the same thing. If so, we included all of them. You may choose those that work best for you.

*All the Stuff You Need to Know About RVing* will provide a solid foundation for those who are thinking about and exploring the RV lifestyle. It will also aid those who are already RVing and seeking to buy another RV that more closely matches their chosen way of travel. Seasoned RVers will enjoy reading the hints and ideas they can incorporate into their RV travels to ease the daily journey. With new products and more information on RVing, some will read this book to discover, in a practical way, how to improve or maintain their RV.

We hope that all will find this book useful and we know you will read it and often refer to it. We recommend that it becomes the book that you regularly re-read. There are over 500 hints. Some may not apply to you today, but as you progress in the RV lifestyle, you will pick up this book and find that hint that solves today's problem.

We hope you enjoy our book, *All the Stuff You Need to Know About RVing,* and will recommend it to your friends.

Go RVing, and enjoy.

Ronald E. Jones
Robert G. Lowe

# Introduction

## *Look Here First...*

This book will help you.

First, this book is for two different groups.

One is first-time buyers—those totally new to RVing but possibly not new to camping. The information throughout this book is specifically directed at camping "on wheels" and definitely leans toward the larger RVs.

The second group is experienced RVers who want to get into a larger or different type of RV. This could be someone that may own a pickup camper but wants to move to a 5th wheel, or that may own a towable unit (5th wheel or travel trailer) and may want to move to a motorhome, or someone that owns a gas motorhome and wants to move to a diesel pusher.

This book will help. Much of the information is usable in virtually every RV.

We have included over 500 ideas and suggestions. We numbered about 400 of them so you can easily reference any item. The rest are tucked into the narratives. You will learn...

- How to drive
- How to pack
- How to live
- How to hook up
- How to unhook
- How to live without hooking up
- How to get it home the first time!

- How to dump
- How to maintain
- How to cross a border
- Inside stuff
- Outside stuff
- Extra stuff you can buy
- Safety stuff

Some suggestions are quick and easy. Some are lengthy and expensive. Some are applicable to virtually every camper on wheels. Some are very specific.

Whether you are full time, part time, or only wish you had time, this book will help!

# Why Do I Need To Know This...

The unique RV lifestyle is not something you naturally learn living in an apartment or house. Just think, when was the last time your non-RV friends had to hook up a sewer hose or crank down their TV antenna before driving away? RVing is different—regardless of whether you are on a short trip or living in one full time.

Ron got the idea for this book from three places—first, from close friends with no RV; second, from participating in various RV e-mail groups and rallies; and third, from trying to find information before he and Sandy began full-timing.

First, Ron and Sandy have close friends, a couple, that planned to purchase their very first RV having just retired and put their house up for sale. Their intention was to travel extensively and maybe full time for a while.

This couple asked us at least 40,000 questions about what to do and how to do it—everything from how we stored canned goods to what is "grey" water to why "fast idle" a diesel engine to how we get e-mail. Even when we were traveling, we would trade e-mails with them—answering still more questions. These were all great questions and resulted in numerous get-togethers and lively dinners. We always had a great time. We had the chance to talk about our lifestyle and they just wanted to know—everything!

Second, on many Internet groups, there are numerous and regular posts with questions that often start something like, "We just bought our first RV and …" or "We are waiting for delivery of our new diesel and…" or "My steps are sticking and…." People want and need help—they have spent (or are spending) their money—it's important.

Third, when getting ready to full-time, Ron looked at many books, spent countless hours on RV websites, joined various clubs and read their materials, talked with dealers, attended trade shows, subscribed to the magazines, joined various e-mail groups, and traded many messages with experienced RVers.

All that information proved that no matter how much experience a person has—with the huge number of coaches and models and styles—it isn't enough! While there are a number of books on the market written by individuals or the classic husband-and-wife team, their information is simply limited—not bad, just limited. So, during all our research, certain individuals seemed to stand out—regularly offering good, solid advice on a variety of subjects. Several helped. We thank them all.

Collective wisdom is always good.

# *How to Use this Book...*

This is not a novel about RVing.

This is not a "How to Buy an RV" book.

This book is better used as a kind of non-technical "technical" manual that contains things that are really helpful, make it easier to get started, will make your RVing life a bit easier, will possibly help you out of trouble at some point, and are just nice to know!

We attempted to stay away from brand names but have included a few out of necessity. We have photographed real RVs and real accessories being used in real situations. When brand names appear in photographs, this should not be construed as a recommendation, but merely an illustration. No RV manufacturers were contacted during the writing of this book.

We have offered many suggestions that we hope are beneficial to your lifestyle in an RV. Some are facts. Some are hints. Some are suggestions. Some are rumor. Some work. Some may not (for you).

There are two authors and we asked spouses, friends, sales reps, campground owners, and many other RVers for their suggestions. We often ended up with several ways to accomplish the same thing. If so, we included all of them. You choose which ones work best for you.

We did not organize by RV size or type as much of the information applies to all. Obviously, if you find yourself reading something that simply does not apply to you, move on! The next item may be just what you need. We continuously numbered the items so it is easy to ask about or refer to one.

We thought it best to set it up by functional area. With that, the major sections are…

- *Getting Ready to Drive and Driving Stuff*
- *Stuff Inside the Coach*
- *Outside Stuff while Parked*
- *All the Other Stuff You Need to Know*
- *Crossing Borders*

Enjoy!

# A Word on Safety and Caution...

Portions of this book involve information about the driving, towing, and handling of RVs. Since driving the RV is one of the uses for it, and since driving any vehicle has an element of risk, it is incumbent on the RVer (you) to be aware of the safety issues, be aware of the laws, and practice safe driving techniques.

This book is not meant to be a "driving" course, nor driving instruction, nor even suggestions for how to drive a RV. It does suggest ideas for learning and practicing maneuvers in an off-road environment such as a large parking lot. These ideas will apply to both drivable and towable RVs. These ideas will also apply to both the driver and copilot—the other adult who will share the driving and responsibility for safety.

RV drivers are considered among the safest in the world. This may be due to age, experience, or factors such as the fact that they are driving their vehicle and home together. Simply, a driving mistake or error will likely be costly in both money and health.

Be safe!

# *About the Authors...*

**Ron Jones** has been camping on wheels since 1962 when he purchased a small tent-trailer and immediately spent two weeks in the Great Smokey Mountains National Park. Through the years, he has owned pick-up campers, Type C, Type B (homemade), and  Type A coaches, plus camped in tents, tent trailers, and travel trailers. He and Sandy (spouse) are fulltimers and are on the move quite a bit in their 42-foot (12.8 m) diesel pusher. They covered approximately 28,000 miles (45,000 km) their first year of fulltiming and didn't make it to Alaska.

Ron is known as "Dr. J" on various e-mail groups. He frequently posts suggestions, offers help, and shares new ideas with members.

Ron is retired (a lot)! He is retired Army (medical, 1970), retired Senior Professor in Engineering Technology at the University of North Texas, and retired publisher (RonJon Publishing, Inc.). Ron's hobbies are traveling, cooking, photography, and writing.

**Bob Lowe** began camping with his parents in a small travel trailer in the early 1960s. He ventured out alone with a tent strapped to his motorcycle in 1966. The lure of the outdoors continued and when GMC introduced their revolutionary  motorhome in the early 1970s, he dreamed of traveling by motorhome.

After camping with his family in two pop-up trailers throughout Southern Ontario, Canada, he and his wife Jane began planning two cross-country trips and bought their first motorhome, a Type C, in 1989. They have progressed through two Type A's and currently own a 39-foot (11.9 m) diesel pusher. They have logged over 180,000 kilometres (112,000 miles) traveling by motorhome throughout North America, while still actively employed.

Other motorhome owners often seek Bob's expertise and he frequently provides technical advice on Internet e-mail groups. Bob served for $3 \frac{1}{2}$ years as the Editor of the Bounder Beacon, a bimonthly, 32-page newsletter read by approximately 3,000 Bounder motorhome owners. Bob has been their Technical Editor for seven years. He operates an Internet-based RV parts business focused on motorhome safety equipment and supplies (www.rv-partsplus.com) and is a Commercial Investment Real Estate Broker.

Bob's hobbies include photography, 12-volt electronics, traveling, and motorcycling.

# Section

*Getting Ready to Drive and Driving Stuff*

Recreational vehicles (RVs) come in two types: towable and drivable. Towable RVs are available in two configurations, including:

**The travel trailer**… is pulled behind a vehicle. The vehicle and travel trailer are connected by a hitch. You can use a car or truck for towing travel trailers.

**The 5th wheel**… is also pulled behind a vehicle but it requires a special type of hitch that is mounted in the bed of the truck. You cannot tow a 5th wheel RV with a car.

"Drivable" RVs are available in three "classes" or "types." Although there is some overlap of available sizes, from smallest to largest, they are available in three types.

**Type B**… RVs are "van-shaped" and will handle just like that big car, big SUV, or pickup truck since they are usually built on a van chassis.

A Type B is the smallest of the drivable coaches.

**Type C**… has the "van" cab and a trailer-like rear section. It is distinguishable by the classic front sleeper—typically one bed is built to extend out over the cab of the vehicle on many models. These RVs range from 22 to 30+ feet (6.7–9+ m) long and are taller than the Type B. Type C RVs require more driver attention to height and length (especially when turning, parking, and backing up).

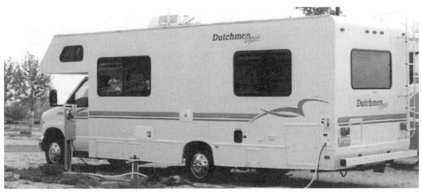

A Type C is the middle sized coach.

**Type A**… motorhomes are full-sized rigs featuring the RV body built on a separate chassis. This type also includes bus conversions. These motorhomes usually start at around 30 feet (9 m)—twice the length of your normal car or pickup truck—and range up to 45 feet (13.7 m) in length!

The largest, the Type A motorhome is a great way to travel and live.

All three types are drivable but each has their own particular uniqueness and challenges as a moving vehicle. For example, add a tow car to a 35-foot (10.7 m) Type A and you instantly have a total length of about 55 feet (16.8 m)—making the overall length close to **four times the length** of a normal car!

The following suggestions don't apply to all RVs but the larger your unit, the more applicable they will likely be. Since the Type B is the most similar to a "normal" vehicle (in size), you will have the shortest learning curve. If you have never driven a 40-foot (12.2 m) Type A diesel pusher, your learning curve will be greater.

---

We have used the following metric conversion conventions throughout the book

m = Metre

cm = Centimetre

m = Millimetre

Km/H = Kilometre per hour

Kg = Kilogram

kPa = Kilopascal

---

---

As with all sections of this book, if the information applies to you, that's great, use it. If the information does not apply to you and your coach, read on.

---

# Learning to Drive Your RV

Today's motorhome is a large vehicle and should be driven by safe and competent drivers.

Driving a RV is different. Therefore, the vehicle must be made ready for you to drive or tow by adjusting virtually everything necessary including the seat, mirrors, and steering wheel, among others. These personal adjustments must be made each time you change drivers. Driving a vehicle is different from just operating a vehicle.

Operating a vehicle assumes that a person can do those things necessary to make it go and stop—but little else. Regardless of your experience, you are just "operating" any vehicle when you first drive it!

Consider this scenario…

You are at the RV dealership, have picked out a great looking coach—perhaps a new, 36-foot (11 m), diesel pusher—and the sales person says, "Let's take it for a drive." Fine," you say, "let's do it."

The sales person will typically have to drive it off the lot (due to insurance liability) and, having done this before, will know where there is a place close by to pull off so that you can drive. The sales person will pull over, put it in Neutral, set the brake, and say, "It's your turn."

You sit down in the driver's seat, adjust the seat, your mirrors, take a deep breath, and are ready to…?

If you have not had experience driving a larger coach, truck, or other vehicle, you will have a lot to learn. It's all "learnable" and you just have to do it! If you have some experience driving larger vehicles, great! It will help.

Of course, you could observe other drivers but it is difficult to know which ones. Often, it is suggested that you watch the truck (semi tractor/ trailer) drivers. Sure, they are among the most experienced— but their rig is different. The  semi trucks are "articulated," that is, they are hinged near the front (just behind the cab). This allows them to turn in a smaller radius than many of the larger motorhomes and provides far greater maneuverability than a larger motorhome. Consider this… watch the semi drivers if you are going to drive a trailer-type RV such as a 5th wheel.

The only RV that closely matches the configuration of a semi truck is the large 5th wheel camper. This unit is pulled behind a pickup (or larger) truck. The physical connection (a hitch) is located in the bed of the truck immediately behind the cab—again, similar to a semi tractor/trailer. This allows 5th wheelers to maneuver into spaces difficult or impossible for larger motorhomes.

### *It's Like a Bus...*

Making a tight, right or left turn in a larger motorhome is an unusual experience (seriously). Like a bus, big coaches have the ability to turn in a smaller radius than many other vehicles. If they could not do this, you could not make a simple right turn onto a relatively narrow street without running over the curb with the rear wheels.

You may hear or read (especially from sales information) that a Type A coach has, for example, a "50-degree" steering angle. This is the maximum angle (measured from straight ahead) that you can turn the wheels and is correctly called the "cramp angle." This feature is common on larger coaches.

The cramp angle controls the "turning radius." Turning radius is measured in distance (feet/metres), not degrees. Turning radius is also affected by wheelbase (a measure from front to rear wheels).

Knowing the exact cramp angle will not help in actual driving situations. However, understanding that this feature will force you to maneuver the coach differently than a "normal" car or light truck will

You will always have to negotiate some construction as you travel.

help you get out of tight spots where sharp turns are necessary. You will frequently be required to turn into a variety of situations (narrow streets, parking lots, driveways, etc.) and a better understanding of this greater maneuverability will increase your driving ability and safety.

It is becoming common that larger motorhomes are built with a "tag axle." This is a second rear axle, with single wheels, set directly behind the normal dual-wheeled axle.

A tag axle is a second axle, with single wheels on each side, positioned directly behind the rear dual-wheel axle. Most tag axles can be raised off the ground when backing or turning. It will automatically lower when the vehicle goes into second gear moving forward.

The purpose of the tag axle is two-fold. First, it will provide additional stability to the rear end by having another two tires on the road—a total of six tires in the rear.

Second, and most important, the tag axle increases the load carrying capacity of the rear of the coach. Most tag axles can be raised up—where the tires will completely clear the road. Doing this actually shortens the wheelbase (measured from front to rear wheels) of the coach. A shorter wheelbase means a tighter turning radius—thus increasing the ability to get in and out of tighter spaces—a real plus in larger coaches.

If the tag axle can be raised, it will remain up in reverse and until second gear is reached when traveling forward. It will automatically lower again to provide stability.

# Driving Practice and Practice Driving...

**A Serious Thought**... When you purchase that RV, **you have to drive it away** from the dealership. Rarely, do they deliver! Are you ready? Have you looked at the potential obstacles between the dealership and where you are going to park it the first night? Depending on where you live, you need to know that you can drive the coach where you want it to be. Check for narrow streets, tight turns, obstacles overhead (tree limbs, wires, signs, canopies, underpass heights), and weight maximums for older smaller bridges. Plus, when you get it home (or wherever), is there enough room to park it—even temporarily?

Before taking your rig out for that first drive, read and review the driving hints provided in the chapter entitled *Driving Suggestions*. At first, on several occasions, practice driving your coach **without the towed car** (toad). Learn what you can and practice those maneuvers with the coach only. Then, when you are a bit more comfortable, hook up the toad.

After hooking up the toad, practice again—all the forward maneuvers and turns—you must not back up with  the toad attached. Yes, it will be different. Attaching that additional 16-foot (4.9 m) long, two-ton, $10,000–$30,000+ object behind you that is not visible in your mirrors, will make a difference. Practice again. Practice until you can make those turns without the toad running over the curb, too. Note: Never backup with the toad attached—damage will occur!

# Try This When Learning to Drive Your RV

1. Have someone take you and the copilot to the dealership to pick up your new coach. It's fine to take the toad to check the hookup if needed. Then unhook before you drive away that first time. The copilot should ride with you the first few times to help watch during those "real" drives. Have that "someone" drive the toad while you two enjoy your new RV.

Rain and overcast weather increases safety issues. Drive accordingly. Be safe.

2. **Take a bus ride**! The larger coaches actually turn "like a bus" and pivot off their rear wheels. That is, the front of the vehicle must be driven straight out (what appears to be too far into the intersection) **before you turn the wheels**.

   A rule of thumb is to pull straight into the intersection until your hips are aligned with the edge of the lane you are turning into. On a right turn, for example, pull straight into the intersection, look to the right until you can see the right edge of the lane you are turning into (it will be aligned with your hips). Turn your wheels maximum and go. Doing this will likely prevent your rear wheels from hitting the curb. Doing this will also tend to startle the people sitting in the lane going in the opposite direction closest to where you are turning in. Since you are pulling out farther than a normal vehicle, and then turning toward them, it will appear to them that you will hit their vehicle as you are turning.

   By going up and over the curb, you could damage your coach, tires, and the light or utility pole at the intersection. Watch your lower mirror when turning and stop if you come too close to the curb. It is far better to spend a few minutes correcting the situation than it is to spend weeks waiting for body parts at a repair shop. Those others drivers that you delay will likely never see you again—so make the prudent decision rather than rushing.

   Of course it takes practice, but first, take a bus ride (in any city, at airports, on most large college campuses). Observe the bus driver while they maneuver the bus—especially the turns. Sit up front and watch carefully. It will be a worthwhile trip.

3. Learn to get out of tight spots. Assume you pull into a big grocery parking lot. You carefully park back, away from the cars, go in, buy groceries, and come out. Someone has parked right in front of you! Can you get out? Sure, you can unhook the toad, back up, rehook up, and go. However, there's another way.

Learn the exact space you need to maneuver. Using that big, empty parking lot again, stop the coach, put it in park, and turn your drive wheels to the **extreme left**. Go out and stand in front of the center of your coach—stand about two arm's length away.

Practice maneuvering out of a tight space. With wheels at maximum left and someone standing two-arms length in front of the coach, creep (slowly).

Have the driver **creep** forward (as slowly as possible) keeping the wheels turned to the extreme left. They should miss the copilot (barely). By doing this, you will know the real distance you need to clear an object in front of you.

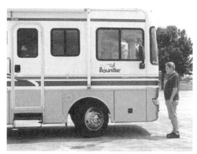

You should miss (we hope) and will learn exactly what clearance you must have to get out of a tight space such as when someone parks directly in front of you in a parking lot.

4. Practice correct turning techniques with your coach. You need to establish a "point of reference" to judge when you can start your turn (actually start

turning the wheels). For a right turn, one good place is to find a reference point on the passenger-side window frame. Until you are comfortable judging this, put a piece of masking tape on the window frame as your reference point to begin the turn.

There are various reference points to use and these depend on your coach's turning radius. Some drivers do not turn their wheels until their hips are opposite where they want them to be in the lane after the turn. On smaller RVs, the front bumper is that reference.

Incorrect steering techniques will cause you to frequently hit the curb with the rear wheels. This will cause damage to the tires, as the sidewalls of the tires are relatively thin when compared to the tread. Tire damage is dangerous and expensive!

5. Use your orange rubber traffic cones and practice turns, judging distance, and maneuvering the coach in a large, empty parking lot. A large church parking lot during mid-week is a good place to practice. It's better to find out you are having trouble backing into a simulated camping space than a real one. While you are practicing, try some U-turns, too.

Using rubber cones to practice driving, judging distance, backing, and turning is an excellent way to become more skilled and competent.

After you feel comfortable doing this, take the coach out for a drive on some two-lane streets—an industrial park is great for this since the streets accommodate large trucks. Often, these businesses close late afternoon and other traffic in the industrial park may be light or nonexistent. Practice some real turns on real streets. Be sure the copilot practices this, too.

6. Practice all this again at night. You will be surprised!

7. Try to find a private, little-used, paved road, out of town. Stop the coach. Check for traffic! Now, floor it in what could be considered an emergency get-away—think of a scenario such as you have just robbed a bank or your copilot just had a heart attack! Do this. You need to know.

   If possible, also do this at the foot of a hill—the steeper the better. No hills where you live? Then look for an on-ramp that has an incline.

8. Using the same private, paved road, carefully staying in your lane (and going about 20 mph—35 Km/H), jerk the steering wheel and immediately change lanes. Use the scenario as though you were swerving to miss a child on a bicycle.

   Do this at 30 mph (50 Km/H). Do it again at 40 mph (65 Km/H).

   Why? These are all typical in-town speeds. Understand what your coach can do in emergency situations before the actual emergency happens.

9. Find your overswing (truckers often call this "overhang swing"). The rear corner of your coach actually swings out when you make a sharp turn—in either direction. You must know this or you will wipe out objects too close to you and damage the rear corners of your RV.

You can do this in a wide driveway since there is only a tiny bit of actual driving. Align your coach's passenger side with the straight edge of the driveway. Be sure to mark the position of the rear of the coach and the center of the rear wheel position. Then the process is the same as in a parking lot.

Align cones (rock, can, or mark) with the rear of the coach and center of the rear wheel (use front **dual** wheel position if you have a tag axle)

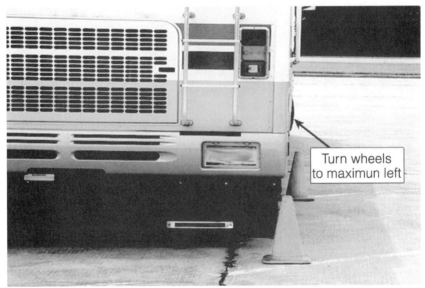

Turn wheels to maximun left

Looking from the rear.

Notice the rear corner of the coach swings out during the turn

Keep wheels turned to maximum left

Measure from cone to edge of coach to find overswing

When creeping (driving **slowly**) through your test, have the copilot stop you when the rear of the coach swings out to maximum width. Then measure from the first cone (mark, etc.) to the edge of the coach. You **must** have this clearance space when turning.

How important is overswing? Very! Significant and costly damage can result from not knowing or not allowing for overswing.

10. Find your U-turn space. Measure the distance needed from side to side you must have to make a U-turn (you want to turn as tight as possible—this is a "get out" maneuver). Assume you turned into a blind parking lot (one where you cannot see the exits nor available space before you enter) and now you have to get out.

Go back into that church parking lot, pull your coach over to the far right side to easily make a U-turn. With the drive wheels straight, set a cone to the right of the front, passenger-side wheel a distance a bit farther out than your overswing.

Put the parking brake on. Turn your wheels maximum left. Release the brake and start your turn. Keep those wheels turned left. Slowly creep through the U-turn.

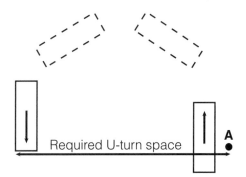

Required U-turn space

Your minimum U-turn space must include the actual turning radius plus your overswing. The real "measure is from the end of the turn to overswing distance (**A**).

When the front, passenger-side corner is at a point in the turn that is maximum distance from where you started, set another cone there.

Move the coach out of the way and measure from marker to marker. This is the absolute minimum distance you need to U-turn your coach. The next time you enter a really tight, blind parking lot, you can measure the U-turn space you need. It works.

Don't assume you can just unhook the toad and easily get out—your required U-turn space does not change whether you are towing or not. However, while unhooking the toad does allow you to back up, this can also be very tricky—and may even be a more difficult maneuver—in a tight parking lot.

11. Find your front blind spot. There is an area directly in front of all vehicles that is a blind spot—it is **physically impossible to see** in this area while sitting in the driver's seat. This area increases with the size of the RV. It is most prevalent in Type A coaches where this blind spot can be large enough to **hide kids, grocery carts, or even a small car!**

Your line of sight—from your eyes to your copilot's toes—is critical in determining how much "blind" area you have in front of your particular coach. Set this up carefully at any campground or parking area.

To find your front blind spot, sit in the driver's seat. Have your copilot stand, facing you, outside in front of the coach. You must look through the windshield just over the top of the dash—so you can see their waist in the lowest part of the windshield. Then, have them step backward slowly until you can see their toes—then they stop. Mark the spot where their toes are and measure from the front of the coach to the mark. This is your blind spot. You cannot see anything in the area from the front of the coach out to a distance equal to the marked spot.

Measure from the toes to the coach. This is your front blind area. You simply cannot see in this area while sitting in the driver's seat. Therefore, you or the copilot must check before driving or you could wipe out a few grocery carts or worse, an expensive car!

The height of the driver does make a difference. Two tests confirmed the following:

| Driver height | Blind area distance in front of coach |
|---|---|
| 6 ft. 3 in.  (1.91 m) | 20 feet  (6.1 m) |
| 5 ft. 2 in.  (1.57 m) | 25 feet  (7.62 m) |

Individual drivers must be aware of their personal blind spot and that this area changes with each driver.

# Things To Do Up Front for Pilot and Copilot

12. When it's your turn to drive and you move into the driver's seat, sit down and adjust everything to fit you before you drive away (the seat itself, mirrors, beverage, etc.). Driving a new coach takes all of your concentration. Be as ready as possible before you go.

13. Adjust your convex mirrors to allow both you and the copilot to see down along side your coach so that cars cannot be in a totally blind spot. Once set, the convex mirrors usually do not have to be moved. Note: Items in the convex mirror are closer than you think. Do not use them to judge distance!

You will use the large mirrors—even in the rain.
Note: the lower convex mirror shows a much wider field of view.

14. Having your mirrors adjusted correctly is crucial to being a safe driver. Adjust the large "normal" mirror so that about one-quarter of the inside portion (nearest the coach) is taken up with the side of your RV. Then set the Earth's horizon about $^2/_3$ to $^3/_4$ of the distance from the bottom. Each driver will need to readjust every time you trade drivers. This is a quick and simple task with powered mirrors.

15. If windshield or side-window reflections are a problem—especially at night, use a dark colored, non-reflective cloth (like polar fleece) to cover your dash to prevent reflections. It needs to be washable. Get two pieces instead of one large one so it will be a bit more manageable.

16. Many of the rear-view monitors found on motorhomes will adjust automatically or they will have settings (a switch) for day usage and night usage. Change the setting as needed. Using the night setting will greatly reduce the glare and  A rear view monitor is ideal for viewing directly behind you. will be easier on your eyes when driving at night or heavily overcast days. This will be similar to decreasing the brightness of your dash lights.

17. Some rear-view cameras may be adjusted and may have a wide-angle lens that enables you to actually see a part of the traffic lanes beside yours—on both sides as well as farther behind. If so, you may also

see along the lower part of other vehicles as you pass them. For example, you might be able to see only the bottom half of their tires or a lower portion of the front fender or bumper. Then you should also be able to see when you have cleared that vehicle, when passing. Of course you need to have additional clearance before you pull back into the driving lane ahead of the other vehicle. However, just being able to use the rear-view monitor to verify when you have cleared is a safety factor.

18. If one of the drivers has difficulty reaching the gas pedal, look into having a left-foot gas pedal installed. These are available at stores specializing in adaptive equipment for the disabled. Most of these companies can also install it for you or direct you to centers that specialize in installing this equipment.

This left-foot gas pedal is closer to the driver's seat and ends up approximately the same relative distance as the brake pedal. Therefore, the left pedal is a bit more accessible to the driver.

A "left pedal drive" can be installed in any vehicle.

Sure, it will take some effort to be comfortable but worth it in the long run for driving comfort. As was suggested earlier—practice, practice, practice! Find that lonely, private road or large empty parking lot and practice.

The left-foot gas pedal folds down flat on the floor when the next driver takes over. It can also be used in the "up" position as it is simply "floating" on the normal, right-hand gas pedal.

19. Many coaches are now equipped with adjustable gas and brake pedals. Ask about this option if you need this feature.

20. Consider enrolling in an RV driving school or at minimum, a safety seminar. Driving schools may be found by searching the Internet, checking with dealers, or contacting various RV organizations and clubs.

21. In the interest of safety, it is recommended that you purchase and understand how to use the following:
    - Any State- or Provincial-mandated safety equipment that you must carry by law.
    - Two to four orange traffic cones—they are handy to have. Taller ones are easier to see.
    - Four emergency flares
    - A 6-volt flashlight or a rechargeable 12-volt portable lantern.

22. Don't "bury" your safety equipment in the deepest recesses of your coach. If stopped, you could be required to show it. More importantly, you will need it in an emergency. Know where it is stored. Make it easy to get to.

# *Driving Suggestions*

23. Try to hit speed bumps straight on (both wheels over at the same time) and very slowly. If you drive over them at an angle (one wheel over slightly ahead of the other), your coach will rock back and forth, from side to side, especially in the back.

    Even going dead slow (creeping), driving over the speed bumps at an angle may cause the coach to rock enough to actually cause things to fly out of the upper cabinets! This is true with the small speed bumps, too. This will also be the case if one side of your wheels hits a depression or pothole commonly found in some of the truck stop lots and campgrounds, the small bumps going up into driveways and parking lots, and the rain gutters built into the cross streets, especially in the south. Driving dead slow with frequent braking is the only answer.

24. You will run into wind gusts occasionally. Crosswinds hitting a large, flat object (the big, flat side of your RV) will naturally cause some swerving. Driver over steering (over compensating) is often the

result and will likely compound the swerving. Truckers suggest using one hand on the steering wheel to steer the coach in extremely heavy crosswinds to prevent over steering. Keep

Driving in the west is a wonderful experience. Yes, there are real dust storms, too.

the other hand lightly touching the steering wheel in preparation for emergencies.

25. As a large transport approaches and overtakes you in gusty wind conditions, you may find that turning the wheel slightly toward the transport truck to offset the effect of the wind force created by the truck allows you to maintain your straight-ahead driving position.

26. Dragging the rear end, especially while towing the toad with the hitch attached, is not good. This is a common way to cut or damage your safety cables.

A simple drive-by or careful observation of the drag marks left by others is a giant clue that you, too, will likely drag.

Notice the dip coming out of the parking lot onto the street. When towing, if both rear wheels hit this depression at the same time, you will likely drag the hitch. This is especially true if you use a drop receiver on your hitch.

Crossing depressions or ditches (very common when coming out of a parking lot or at some cross streets) is the prime place where this happens. There are two driving maneuvers to prevent this from happening.

**Here's the first trick**... Approach the depression as **straight as possible** and keep your wheels pointing **straight forward** until both front wheels are down into the depression as far as possible. Then stop. Turn your wheels as far as possible **before moving the coach**. Then drive out **slowly**.

Following this procedure will cause the rear wheels to pass through the lowest part of the depression at slightly different times. This, in turn, causes the rear end of the coach (where your hitch is located) to literally stay up, at a higher point above the pavement, and the result is no drag.

The one negative in doing this procedure is that you need lots of time and little cross traffic. You literally have to put the front end of your coach into the lane, then stop, and then maneuver out very slowly. You will need ample time, as this must be done slowly.

An innocuous-looking entry into a strip mall parking lot.

Now you can see the steep angle of the car coming out of this parking lot on the same exit. This steep angle will cause you to drag.

**Here's the second trick**... Cross the depression at an angle to enter traffic. Doing this creates the effect of the rear wheels entering the depression at different times. If you have the space available, this is the easier of the two maneuvers.

Notice the front end of the car going down into the bottom of this dip at the entrance to a parking lot. This is your first clue that you should not go there or you will drag.

As the car's rear wheels hit the dip, the rear end of the car comes closest to dragging. Your coach's rear overhang is likely 2-3 times longer than the car's overhang. This is your second clue not to enter this lot at this particular entrance. Notice the up-angle as the car moves into the lot. Seeing the car enter the dip (pointing down) and exit the dip (pointing up) is a sure sign that you will drag.

27. Don't pump your air brakes. (Brakes activated by your brake pedal are also commonly called "service brakes.") Pumping actually releases and reduces the available air used for braking. This is exactly opposite what many drivers were taught. Pumping brakes in a normal vehicle (car or pickup truck) was considered correct practice for years—this is not true with antilock braking systems (ABS), nor air brakes.

When you need to use your service brakes, step on the pedal and use continuous braking pressure, without totally releasing your foot. Changing to a slightly lighter or heavier pressure is fine once you are on the brake pedal. Using a constant braking pressure takes practice.

Air brakes and the air system require maintenance. Check your owner's manual.

28. You have to drive in three dimensions—not like your basic car or pickup truck. As always, you are concerned with the front, rear, and sides of your vehicle, but the motorhome is very tall as well—some are

This quiet neighborhood street has two problems for RVers. First, the low, overhanging tree branches. Second, the stop sign is set too close to the lane and you may hit it with your mirror.

over 12 feet (3.7 m) tall! As you drive the motorhome, you must be aware of this third dimension—height.

Air conditioners, TV antennas, satellite dishes, and solar panels are all mounted on the roof of your coach. You cannot see them while driving. However, **you must be aware that they are up there**—especially when driving under such things as overhanging tree limbs, wires, signs, and canopies to name a few. Knocking your air conditioner off your roof is an expensive and time-consuming mistake.

There are many items mounted to the roof of the RV. You cannot see these when driving.

Right after you get your coach, park it on a level area, and make sure your air bags are inflated. Climb onto the roof and, working with the copilot,

Shows overall height of coach in both feet and metres.

measure the exact height of your coach—no extra—the exact height. Write this down, post it on the dash.

Memorize it. It is important. You **cannot** drive through a space this high. Disregard what the manufacturer or sales person said about your clearance height, measure for yourself. It's your air conditioner up there—knock it off if you want.

If you are driving a diesel coach with air ride suspension and have a life and death emergency, you may be able to make it through a space your exact driving height by dumping your air bags. Generally, this is only 3–4 inches (7–10 cm) of extra clearance.

Mentally add 6 inches (15 cm) to your exact height. Write that down too and memorize it. You can—in an emergency—drive through a space this high **if their posted clearance is correct** and if it is an emergency! Plus, dumping your air bags will help a bit more. Remember, use this procedure only if it is an emergency and do not turn your wheels until you have re-inflated your suspension. This is still too close for comfort!

Pay attention to clearance signs and hope they are correct.

At minimum, give yourself an extra foot of room. Life will be better and stress will be less. Finally, try not to go under canopies if they are not marked.

29. While driving on an interstate highway, occasionally note what mile marker you are passing. These are the small vertical green signs along side the highways and at the exits. Consider this...

While RVing, you will see many unique sights. Here is the largest number on any mile marker in the U.S. It is located on I-10, eastbound, leaving Texas at the last exit before entering Louisiana.

- If you have trouble and have to stop, when you call for emergency service, giving your mile marker location will help them find you.

- Most road atlases will have mile markers noted on them. Knowing your mile marker will help you find how far you are from the next rest stop or exit.

---

**Two special notes**...

California is the only state that does not use mile markers. They use some type of small white marker that relates to distances within that particular county. However, we understand that they are now installing "normal" mile markers in the state. This will be very helpful when they finish.

Exit numbers **do not always match mile markers**. Some states use a consecutive numbering system for exits, e.g., Exit 1, Exit, 2, etc. Some states/provinces are changing from the "non-matching" system to the "mile marker" system. You may see something like "Exit 142" with a second small sign with "Old 19" or the like on it.]

30. For emergency stops, in what is commonly known as "the middle of nowhere," your GPS (Global Positioning System) will have your exact coordinates. Giving these coordinates to many emergency service organizations will be extremely helpful, allowing them to pinpoint your location.

31. It is strongly recommended that the driver and copilot share the driving responsibilities. One or the other may become incapacitated and unable to drive. Sharing the driving ensures an extra margin of safety for everyone.

Trade drivers about every $1\,^1/_2$ hours. There are three excellent reasons for this...

- This gives everyone the same opportunity to practice driving the coach.

- Driving a new (at least new to you) unusual vehicle takes serious concentration and effort. All this increases your fatigue. Simply—you get tired.

- When you stop, take 5 minutes to do some fast walking outside the coach. This will decrease the potential for blood clots forming from sitting in one position for long periods of time and thus, decrease the chance for stroke. Plus, it will give you a chance to look at your new coach. Use the walk to both admire your coach and walk around it once to keep an eye on it for any problems.

# Getting Ready to Drive (The Daily Occurrence)

32. Travel with **all** windows closed to keep fumes outside and prevent dust from coming into the living area. Open rear windows especially may suck fumes and odors into the coach.

33. If your coach has driver or passenger window screens, consider removing the driver's screen. A good place to store it is behind the sofa. This will help in paying tolls, crossing borders, etc.

34. Close ceiling vents. There is a roof-mounted cover that fits over roof vents. Installing these will allow you to leave the roof vent open when driving. No rain will come into the coach through the open vent since the cover protects it.

Deflectors are roof mounted over the crank-up roof vents. Leave the vent open even if it is raining.

35. Turn off LP gas appliances (water heater, furnace, and refrigerator) to be safe. Your water will stay hot for a long time. Your fridge and freezer will be just fine for hours and it's okay to occasionally open the fridge door. Your engine cab heater (up front) should provide ample heat while driving in cold weather. Closing a mid-coach door (between living room and bath, for example) can make the dash heater more effective.

36. Put big loose things on the bed—including everything from coffee tables, tray tables, bags of groceries, laundry bags, etc.

37. If you are in a hurry to get going after buying groceries, put the grocery bags in the bathtub and go. A single bag can be put into the sink.

38. Not able to dry the last load of clothes you washed? Set the wet clothes in the bathtub and go.

39. Check that all doors and drawers are latched.

40. Lock the coach door from the inside.

41. If your coach has a diesel, a bit of engine warm-up is recommended when starting cold in the morning. However, diesel engines don't warm up at "normal" idle speed—they must be run at a "fast idle" to generate heat. Check with your dealer or the manual for this fast idle speed.

    Many coaches use the following technique: As soon as you start the cold engine, gently and slowly increase the engine speed by depressing the pedal until you have reached the fast idle rpm setting. Then engage your cruise control (press the button) and gently, slowly let your foot off the pedal. Your engine should remain at the fast idle rpm. (On some rigs, it may be necessary to turn on a switch often located under the dash marked "IDLE INC/DEC" to allow this function to be activated.)

This is an excellent time to bring in slides, put the jacks up, and finalize the last minute details just before pulling out of the campsite.

Note: Many motorhomes are designed so the slides won't operate if the engine is running. If so, bring the slides in early in the departure process. Doing so makes access to the storage bays easier. Then set the engine idle.

# Hooking Up the Toad (Tow Vehicle)

42. Hook up your tow car carefully! Establish a fixed routine such as the tow bar arms first, safety cables next, wiring, and breakaway cable last. When you finish hooking up everything, literally stand up and look—carefully look—at each connection just to ensure it is good and complete. This 15-seconds of safety could save your vehicle. A common campground courtesy rule is not to talk with folks while they are hooking up towed vehicles.

The complete tow-bar assembly is shown, ready to tow.

Many incomplete hookups are a result of you being interrupted by someone or something during the hookup procedure. For example, the person in the next campsite says "goodbye," you look up to acknowledge it, and forget to attach something. It happens. The visual double-check will likely prevent incomplete hookups.

If you get interrupted a second time, do it again. After all, it's only your car! Ask your copilot to double-check the hookup. They may see something you overlooked.

43. Check the lights on the toad periodically (brake lights, turn signals, and running lights) during the trip. **Always check the lights when you first hook it up,** before you drive away, and periodically during the trip. Apply a little dielectric grease (tune-up grease) to the female connections to combat corrosion and enhance conductivity.

Recheck the lights **without** adjusting or jiggling the wiring connections. If the lights are working—fine, your connection is good. If they are not working, you may simply need to tighten the connection. If you frequently find them not working, you may need to replace the wiring connectors or further service your wiring. However, if you jiggle or tighten the connection each time **before** you check the lights, you will never know if the wiring is going bad.

# Backing Up an RV

Backing up a motorhome can be intimidating. However, the following technique will have you parking like a pro in no time. For simplicity, assume that you are trying to park on a paved campsite with a defined edge and a wider entrance apron and you want your motorhome 3 feet (1 m) from the edge.

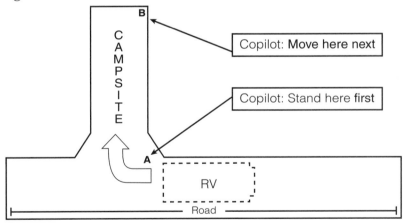

**All RVs pivot from their rear wheels. All you need to do is have the rear wheels in the correct position before backing.** The remainder of the task is simply follow-through.

a. Try to approach your campsite so the site is on the driver's side. This will make parking easier.

b. When approaching your campsite, drive up slowly, check for traffic, and move to the left. Leave about 6 feet (2 m) of space from the edge of the **road**.

c. As you pass the site's entrance, look for a point where the true edge of the paved area would intersect with the edge of the road. (Position A in the figure). Ignore any wider entrance aprons. The copilot should stand at that intersection (A).

d. The copilot should identify a spot on the RV 3 feet (1 m) forward of the wheels.

e. Back up straight and slow. The copilot should signal as that spot passes Position A.

f. Immediately turn the steering wheel as far as possible to guide the coach into the campsite. The driver should stop and wait while the copilot repositions.

g. The copilot should move to the rear of the campsite (Position B) always remaining visible to the driver.

h. Back up slowly turning the steering wheel as needed to straighten the coach. Stop when signaled to do so by the copilot.

44. Tilt your mirrors down to see the lower rear corner of your coach. When backing, your concern is no longer with traffic approaching from the rear but with carefully guiding the rear of your coach into a site.

Use rubber cones to practice backing up. Try to align the rear of the rig with the cone, using only your mirrors.

45. Back up **slowly**.

46. Use both mirrors, your rear camera monitor, and have someone guide you. The guide should stand at the rear, driver's side of your coach and be visible in the driver's side mirror. Never have the guide stand behind the coach. If they cannot see your mirrors, you cannot see them. Ensure they look overhead for any tree limbs or obstacles that you cannot see in the mirrors. It is impossible to see everything around your coach when using only the mirrors and monitor.

Always use someone outside the RV to help guide you when backing.

47. When you drive up to a site you are going to back into, if possible, approach the site and position the RV so you are backing the rear of the coach **toward** the driver side (wheels are turned to the left). Starting from this position allows you to primarily use the driver's mirror plus you can stick your head out the window if needed.

48. When you are outside, guiding the driver, if you cannot see the coach mirrors, the driver cannot see you.

49. **Never** back up with the toad attached.

# Fueling Up

50. If you pull into a truck stop, look for the "Truck Entrance" sign. Don't go in the "car" side—you typically cannot drive from one side to the other without exiting the property. You may find "RV Lanes" and these will have both gas and diesel tanks. Larger rigs may have trouble in these RV Lanes.

51. If you pull into a **busy** truck stop, there will be trucks (tractor/ trailer rigs) waiting in line to get to the pumps. Get in line at one of the pumps. It's okay to shut off your engine but stay in the coach. Be ready to pull forward the moment the vehicle at the pump pulls forward.

Truck stop etiquette means you move your rig forward immediately after refueling. This allows the trucks behind you to start fueling up while you pay.

52. When you pull in to fuel up, turn **off** all LP gas appliances in the coach—that is, no open flames.

---

**Caution**… Before entering a fuel station, turn off all LP gas appliances (refrigerator, water heater, and furnace) at their respective power switches., Most have re-igniter systems that will produce dangerous sparks if you just turn off the LP and not the power.

---

53. Diesel fuel prices are usually shown on truck stop signs in yellow. Gasoline prices are shown in white.

As you look for fuel pricing, diesel is most often shown in yellow.

54. Buy a cheap pair of leather work gloves and use these when handling the diesel pumps and the window washing stuff at the diesel islands—as the gloves become filthy, toss them and get some more.

55. Diesel islands for trucks usually have long-handled window washing squeegees—wash your windows while fueling. Don't forget the driver and passenger windows, mirrors, and headlights.

56. When using diesel islands in truck stops, you can fill from both sides if you have dual fill tubes. Usually the passenger side is a pump only and the gauges, credit card, and info is located on the driver's side. With a "small" tank of less than 150 gallons, **use one pump only** to give you enough time to wash the windshield.

57. Diesel pumps at truck stop islands pump fuel incredibly fast—likely more than twice as fast as a standard gasoline pump—so be careful. Use the pump lock so you won't have to hold it, but set it on the **slowest** setting—it will still pump very rapidly.

58. You **may** have to send the copilot inside to register your credit card with the cashier before they will turn on your pump. There is usually a phone at the pump to connect directly to the cashier—call and ask.

59. Many RVers have the two-way radios. Have the copilot take a radio inside. Let the copilot know you are finished pumping and they won't have to frequently get in line to ask the cashier.

60. Immediately after refueling, unless there are empty pumps, pull your coach forward to clear the islands and allow the vehicle behind you to pull in.

Be sure to pull your rig (including the toad) far enough forward to clear the island for the next vehicle.

Make sure your toad clears, also. An easy way to judge this (remember, your copilot is inside) is to pull the front end of your coach so that it is even with the front of one of the tractor/trailer rigs that has pulled forward in the next lane. They are typically longer than you so you will be okay.

61. Have an old piece of carpet to wipe your shoes on after walking around at the diesel islands. A floor mat will not work. You need a soft, deep-pile cloth to wipe the fuel smudges from your shoe soles.

62. Buy your diesel fuel at a real truck stop. These have high turnover and a high volume of fuel is used.

63. Many truck stops will offer a discount of a few cents for cash.

64. Use only #2 diesel—do not use what is considered the tax-free fuel as this is designed for agricultural or "off road" usage. It is cheaper but you will pay stiff fines if you are caught with it. This grade of fuel is a different color than the standard #2 diesel so it is easy to tell the difference.

# *Temporary Parking*

65. Pull into a large parking lot where you can park your coach and toad across multiple car spaces. Then get out and count the spaces you are covering plus one more in front, so you can drive out. Once you know, you can do a quick count from the driver's seat before you pull into any potential row. Knowing this is extremely handy in a busy, crowded parking lot.

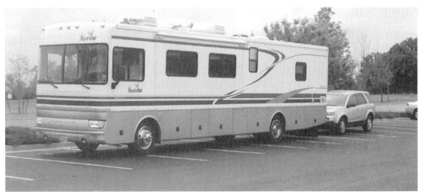

After pulling your rig across the parking spaces, carefully count the number of parking spaces your total rig (coach and toad) needs. You need some space to drive out so add one more. Then you need some space to drive it in. This will likely take about two more. The rig shown here needs 10 total spaces to fit (7 + 1 + 2).

66. When parking across several spaces, make certain your toad's rear end is not sticking out in the traffic lane. It must be inside the lines of the parking spaces as well.

Judge from both front and back. Be sure.

67. Look for fast food billboards that mention bus/truck/RV parking. These billboards may also have a small "bus" or "truck" drawing on them. Those locations should have ample space for your RV.

68. Virtually any truck stop will have ample parking.

69. Use the truck parking areas in rest stops. Don't go into the car parking area unless there is no designation.

70. Staying the night in rest areas may not be allowed. Check for signs. Some rest areas will have security.

Follow the appropriate signs when parking. You are no longer just a simple vehicle that can fit anywhere.

Try to stay where there are plenty of trucks just for

the security of numbers. You will have to put up with the truck engines running all night.

71. Wal-Mart allows free, overnight parking in most locations. It is always best to check with their security or customer service. Do not set up camp here! No awnings, jacks, slides, grills, or lawn chairs! If the greeter or customer service representative does not give you a location to park in, then park as far from the front door as possible. Go in, buy something, and say thanks!

72. Cracker Barrel allows free, overnight parking in locations where they can accommodate bus/RV parking. Most of their billboards will mention bus/ RV parking if they have it. Check with the manager first. Follow the "Wal-Mart Rules." Go in, eat something, and say thanks!

73. Flying J Truck Stops allow free, overnight parking in most locations. Many have a different area that is away from the big trucks. Go in and buy something and say thanks!

# A Special Note Regarding Parking Overnight on Private Business Parking Lots...

Many RVers spend the night in Wal-Mart parking lots, Flying J truck stops, Cracker Barrel restaurant parking lots, and other private businesses. These overnight stays should be just one night's parking, usually arriving in late afternoon or evening and leaving fairly early the next morning. The generosity of these businesses is a wonderful, convenient, and money-saving privilege for many RVers.

Unfortunately, there are those who abuse the privilege by overstaying their welcome, leaving trash scattered around, dumping gray water on the ground, partying under their awnings, etc. Even if the businesses choose to put up with them, there is still a danger of a municipal government passing a "No Overnight Parking" regulation, causing RVers to lose the privilege—and it is a privilege.

There has been a list passed around various RV groups that establish the "rules" for this boondocking privilege. This list has become affectionately known as "Wal-Mart Rules" (shown below). However, it must be noted that **the list was generated by RVers for RVers and is not officially connected with Wal-Mart in any way**.

---

### Attention Campers

We welcome you to our store. You may stay in our parking lot and we appreciate your patronage. While you are here, we request that you observe the following rules of courtesy:

- Please limit your stay to one night. Arriving later in the day, and leaving early in the morning would also help us reduce congestion in our parking areas.

- Please place trash in trash receptacles only.

- Do not empty gray water on the ground or in the sewer drains. If you need to empty your tanks, ask our information desk for the nearest location of an approved dump station.

- Please don't extend awnings, set up chairs and tables, or otherwise make our parking lot appear to be a campground. It can result in a loss of privileges. If you must put down your leveling jacks, be sure to place a large flat board under them to avoid damaging the asphalt parking lot.

- Park so that your generator, if used, doesn't bother our customers.

- Park in areas suggested by our staff or near other RVs. These areas are selected for your safety and for minimal inconvenience to our customers and staff.

If you see others violating these guidelines, please let us know.

Thank you!

---

# Copilot Help is Special Help

74. Copilots can be especially helpful in narrow city driving. One important thing they need to watch for are signs that "lean" into the right-hand traffic lane. These will damage a mirror.

75. The copilot should be reading the map and looking for situations where the driver will need advance warnings about changes in route.

76. The copilot must also provide the extra set of eyes when traveling in difficult situations.

77. Always be scanning the road in advance of where

Both signs lean into the right-hand lane of the street. It is extremely easy to hit these with your right mirror.

you are going for hidden obstructions, police or emergency vehicles stopped on the road side that must be given space (sometimes required by law).

78. If you use a GPS and/or a computer for tracking or planning your trip then the copilot should be confirming that you are on track. The driver must be in control of the vehicle and most concerned about the road and road conditions.

79. The copilot should be concerned about the routing and time and helping to decide when and where to switch positions.

80. In a motorhome, the copilot can assist the driver with refreshments, which must be consumed with care.

81. Establish a set of hand signals and **always use them** (even when using two-way radios!) to guide the driver. Think about it. The driver is looking at you in the mirror, your image is backward (in the mirror), and you tell the driver to go left while backing up. Practice the hand signals back in the church parking lot. If you fail to practice this, you will provide entertainment to the other campers while you are attempting to park your rig.

82. If using the hand-held, two-way radios (the ones you have to hold in your hand and press the button to talk), do not expect the driver to always instantly respond since he or she is probably busy checking the mirrors, rear-view monitor, steering, and braking while trying to back up the coach. It is difficult to stop one of these tasks to pick up a radio and talk.

Use some "outside" help when parking an RV.

83. If you use the two-way radios, be sure to say "Over" when you finish speaking. It is also good practice to say the driver's name regularly when speaking. With the number of people using these handsets in busy RV locations and the limited number of channels available, it is possible to hear someone else and do exactly the opposite of what the copilot wanted. Repeating the driver's name and finishing with "Over" lets the other person know who you are speaking to, when you are finished speaking, and that the other person can now talk (transmit). Without the use of "Over," you will talk over each other and no one can hear anything.

84. Purchase a headset radio that has true, two-way communication (both of you can talk at the same time—like talking on the phone). These are available at some motorcycle dealers or electronics outlets.

Traveling in an RV allows you to take advantage of the scenic wonders—just ahead.

# **S**ection

## *Stuff Inside the Coach*

You have to live in your RV for some period of time. It may be the occasional weekend or full time as many RVers do. Even the largest motorhome is probably smaller than that first tiny apartment you rented—years ago! Surviving for an

You "live" in the RV so daily items are commonly pulled out of storage for use.

occasional weekend is easy enough. Surviving for weeks or months is different. You must be efficient and (at least a bit) organized.

You must be efficient because you cannot stock up with multiples of the same items like you did in your home or apartment. This applies to clothing, food, knickknacks, pictures, and those things we normally live with. You can certainly have some of everything, but you must pick and choose.

You must be a bit organized since you are living in a small space when compared to your home or apartment. Therefore, you cannot have items scattered around casually. Plus, loose items will likely end up on the floor or, worst case, become a projectile when driving.

Some items will need to be stored when driving. The coffee pot is rarely permanently mounted in newer RVs.

As with all sections of this book, if the information applies to you, that's great, use it. If the information does not apply to you and your coach, read on.

# Learning to Live in Your RV

85. Do a "Shakedown Cruise." Take a short trip in your new coach and plan to stay out 2–3 nights—three is better. Your goal here is to "try" everything—all the appliances, the holding tanks, the TV, satellite system, toilet, jacks, awning, sewer hose, etc.—several times for each. It is much better to find any problems before you take a long trip. Problems include items not functioning correctly and you not knowing how to operate the items.

   If you can, try to move every day to another campground in a totally different park to force you to practice hooking up and unhooking everything. It's work but it's worth it. Plan to drive 20–30–40 miles (30–45–60 Km) minimum between parks to give you time to jostle everything around.

86. Allow yourself several full days just to pack the coach the first time. You need time to decide what to take, if it will fit, where you will put it, and how you will remember where it is. The **RV packing rule** is…

   *"Keep anvils low and feathers high."*

That is, pack and store your heavy items in lower compartments, lighter items up higher, and always remember to spread the weight around. Soon after loading, if possible, you should have your coach weighed to ensure you are not overweight on any wheel location. There is additional information about the importance of weighing your RV and how to do it in Section 3.

87. Cabinet doors may pop open when traveling and especially if you have to cross a speed bump. Purchase the "child-proof" latches for cabinets— but not the ones

Exterior "child-proof" latches will prevent cabinet doors from opening while driving.

that attach to the inside of the cabinet door. Get the ones that drape across both cabinet handles where you have matching doors. Latch those doors together when you drive and be sure to go over those speed bumps dead slow.

88. Try using your coach air conditioner(s) when driving rather than your engine air. While it is important to regularly use your engine air conditioner to keep the seals lubricated and performing, using your coach air conditioner(s) will provide good climate control and it will force you to exercise the generator under load, when traveling. With the generator running, you will also be able to run the refrigerator on AC rather than LP gas when traveling.

89. Get one of the magnetic key holders used for hiding keys. Put a **door key, an ignition key, and a fuel door key** inside. Hide it well. Crawl around underneath and find a great hiding place. Cover it with mud or spray paint it to look like the background.

90. Make a list of phone numbers (family contacts, emergency services, coach and chassis manufacturer, dealer, insurance, etc.). Make copies so both the pilot and copilot can carry one, put one up front in the coach, and one in the toad. It is nearly impossible to get to some of this information when stored, for example, under the bed or in a cabinet obstructed by the slide—especially when slides cannot be opened for any reason!

91. When the slides are **not out** is a good time to check to see if you can reach the necessities that may be obstructed when the slides are in. Can you get a jacket or umbrella out of the closet? Can you reach the pet food? Plan where things will be stored so you can adjust as needed before it becomes a problem—on that occasion when a slide will not operate.

92. Learn how to manage your systems by being conservative with your water and electrical usage, especially if you want to boondock or dry camp.

# *Living Room*

You spend a lot of time in the living room—just like in a real house! Therefore, your comfort level is important in your RV. Spend time thinking about how to make this unique space fit your particular lifestyle and needs. It's worth the effort.

93. If your coach has driver and passenger seats that swivel, learn how to adjust them when parked to provide additional seating.

94. Reading lights are notoriously miserable in many RVs. Find one of those inexpensive, small, clip-on light fixtures that use a 60-watt (maximum) bulb. These work fine and can be moved as needed.

95. Check for storage space behind the sofa. Sometimes a short, folding ladder can be stored there.

96. Use the carpet samples (they have a finished edge on them) to put temporary carpet on your entry steps. Cut the sample to step-size and use two-sided carpet tape to hold it down with the finished edge out (it looks better). Toss when dirty.

97. Ask for an rf-type satellite receiver remote control to use in the bedroom. By using an rf-type receiver, it is not necessary to have line-of-sight between the remote and the receiver. With this type of remote, you can change channels with the bedroom door closed.

98. One of the old, plastic, TV tables (short, with wheels) will work well for a coffee table and can be easily moved around as needed. Store it on the bed when driving.

# Satellite Info—TV plus Internet and E-mail

## Overview...

There are two uses for a satellite dish on your coach. Most common is TV reception. The other is access to the Internet and this access automatically includes e-mail.

The small, crank-up satellite dish that comes on most coaches is designed for TV only. Manually positioning this dish is sometimes frustrating. Many people are adept at "finding" the satellite and are happy with the reception. It is

RVers use a variety of styles to set up and steady their satellite dish.

handy to have a Signal Finder meter that connects between the satellite antenna and the receiver. This helps you to locate the correct signal and maximize the signal strength. Excellent reception is available over much of the North American continent. However, the farther you travel north or south, the larger the satellite dish must be. Unfortunately, the manual, crank-up dish on most coaches is one of the smallest.

Many RVers carry a second, portable satellite dish with them that they can set up external to the RV. This second dish is usually mounted on a small tripod and placed on the ground near their coach.

A homemade satellite dish support made from PVC pipe. This is both stable and very portable.

RVers carry this second dish to help ensure they won't be without reception if parked under a tree or some obstacle. If their rooftop dish reception is blocked, they can usually move the second dish to a place where they have a clear line-of-sight to the satellite in the sky. If you carry a second dish, use RG-6 cable (available in electronic stores). This cable is heavier so there is less signal loss. Purchase at least a 50-foot length.

TV reception is readily available through your normal TV antenna unless you are in the proverbial "middle of nowhere." For example, do not expect any TV reception if you are camped near the rim of the Grand Canyon! However, if camped within a reasonable distance from just about any city, you can probably get local channels just fine. Many RVers want to watch TV and satellite reception may be the only solution at times.

To "move up" from the small satellite dish, today, you have choices from two major companies. One company is KVH TracVision and the other is MotoSat. There are a number of differences in their products.

---

This technology is changing rapidly. Additionally, companies offering the equipment and services are frequently changing what they offer. Special "sales" are ongoing. **You must carefully research this area for prices and services.** With the companies making frequent changes, make sure your data (prices and service options) is up-to-date—even two-month old data may be outdated.

---

## For TV Access Only...

One of the two most popular, and becoming commonly available on new coaches, is the KVH TracVision dish. This satellite system is designed for TV reception only—**not Internet**.

The KVH TracVision dish is housed inside a dome and is designed as an "in-motion" system. This means that the satellite dish will operate (it actually rotates inside the protective dome) while the coach is moving—driving down the highway—and you can watch TV. It must be noted that front mounted TVs in drivable coaches are wired so they cannot be used when the ignition key is turned on. Operating a TV viewable by the driver is illegal in most states and provinces. The in-motion satellite dish allows your passengers to watch other TVs in the coach.

MotoSat does not currently offer a lower priced in-motion system for non-commercial users. They do offer high-end systems used by emergency services.

The in-motion dome as seen from the front and roof. A roof-mounted dome contains an in-motion satellite. However, you should note that it is unlawful to operate a television mounted anywhere the driver can see it while driving. Front-mounted TVs are wired to shut off when the ignition key is turned on. In-motion TV is limited to the second TV, most likely located in the bedroom.

## For Internet Usage...

Both companies offer different solutions for Internet access. Purchase of either system will require what many RVers believe to be a considerable investment. However, as more are sold, prices should go down.

Since the TracVision system is for TV only, for access to the Internet, you must add a second, smaller dome called the KVH TracNet. This is a **separate, second, in-motion system used for Internet only**—not TV. Therefore, you must have both domes installed separately in order to access both TV and Internet.

Installing both domes on the rooftop of the coach requires some planning. Additionally, there is a cost for each dome and each installation since the two are separate systems. The TracNet will provide Internet access to your laptop while the vehicle is in motion. You can have your laptop up front while driving.

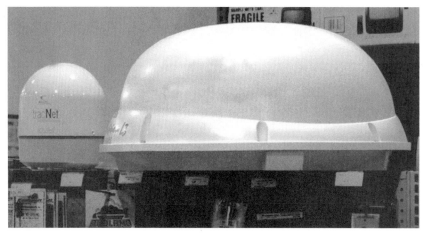

The second, smaller dome is for Internet only. The larger dome is for TV only. Both must be installed on the roof of the RV. Each dome is individually priced and service to each is also individually priced.

The MotoSat mobile satellite systems company sells a product called DataStorm. The DataStorm 2-Way satellite system consists of a dish mounted on the roof of your coach. This dish is **not** an in-motion system and must be raised and lowered (automatically powered) when the coach is parked.

The DataStorm 2-Way satellite system consists of a single dish. However, **this single dish provides access to both TV and Internet, simultaneously.** The DataStorm is typically connected directly to a laptop computer. The computer contains the program for accessing (locking on) the satellite. Simply clicking on a button to "Find Satellite" will cause the dish to raise, aim, lock-on, and test for the best signal. Immediately after locking on, both TV and Internet are accessible.

The MotoSat satellite dish is a large unit when operating. However, it is both a dual satellite TV receiver and Internet connection.

The DataStorm dish folds down onto the top of the coach roof in preparation for moving. The folded height is approximately 8″ and many RVers have these installed behind the forward roof air conditioner. In the folded position, the dish is lower than the air conditioner housing. This provides some additional protection to the DataStorm dish from tree limbs and other overhead obstacles.

The MotoSat satellite dish is about 8-inches tall when stowed—lower than roof-mounted air conditioners.

# TV Access and Costs...

You can get satellite TV in your RV from either of the two major providers in the U.S.—currently Dish Network and DIRECTV. Canadian RVers also have a choice of two providers—Bell ExpressVu or StarChoice. Canadian RVers should note that the factory-mounted or RV dealer-installed dish will not work with StarChoice. You will need to change the LNBF head for it to work, or obtain a StarChoice dish.

If you travel part time, some RVers choose to move the receiver from their house to their coach for local trips. If you travel extensively, you will not be able to receive your regular "local" channels at some distance from your home with the U.S. providers.

To gain local channel access with the U.S. providers, if you full time, you must apply for service. The application process requires that you submit an affidavit (a form) to the satellite company stating that you affirm that the satellite antenna is in a moving vehicle and that it is not intended for use in a "fixed" residence. This process can take several weeks so do it long before a major trip. Check their respective websites or call the companies directly to obtain the correct form.

With approval, you should be able to get your local channels at a range of about 200 miles from your home base. Additionally, approval will provide you access to the major network feeds (channels) from both New York and Los Angeles. If you live in the Midwest, times for your favorite shows will suddenly be different.

While access to the major networks is necessary (if you watch the popular shows), you will have to use your antenna for local channels. Why watch local channels? One important reason is to see the local weather. Your network feeds will have the weather in LA or New York, but not locally.

All providers regularly offer "deals" and pricing is competitive. There are various "packages" that offer a variety of sports, movies, and specialty shows. Carefully select the one that fits your viewing preferences. There is usually a one-year contract required.

A typical deal may include the offer of additional receivers at no extra cost. Using one receiver allows you to receive all the channels in the viewing package you selected but the same program shows up simultaneously on all your TVs and recording devices. If you want to watch two different shows at the same time (one on the front TV and the second on the bedroom TV), you must have two receivers. Having two receivers will also allow you to watch one program and record a different program at the same time on your VCR.

## Internet Access and Costs...

Regardless of the system you choose, there will be an additional monthly charge for Internet access, if available. These charges are separate from the TV packages and may be expensive. Therefore, you must do your research and understand what your costs will be before installing a satellite system.

Currently, two types of packages for Internet access are offered by the companies.

**KVH TracNet**... Users of this system have packages available based on "minutes used"—a program similar to early cell phone plans. You select the level of usage you want and prepay for "X" number of minutes each month. If you exceed the number of minutes in a given month, you are charged an additional "fee per minute" for each minute you run over.

**DataStorm 2-Way**... Users of this system have one option. You are charged a monthly fee for 24/7 (unlimited) access.

# Internet Access with Cell Phones... and WiFi

Most cellular providers offer flat-rate packages for a specific amount of data access time or a "pay as you go" by the minute. You will need an adapter cable that fits your cell phone and connects to your computer's USB port. This setup allows the computer to treat the cell phone as a modem. Access speeds vary and are generally slow—similar to speeds obtained with telephone modems. You will need to configure your e-mail and Internet software to recognize the new cellular modem connection.

Cell phone Internet access saves money and permits you to change rigs without a major extra cost. Since RVers tend to move, slow access speeds, variable service levels, and locations where the cellular signal is too weak for dependable access are the tradeoffs.

With WiFi (wireless), some RVers use a laptop computer and wireless cards to access the Internet. Many campgrounds have installed the wireless service. Plus, there are "hot spots" at service centers, Internet cafes, and electronics stores. Costs vary from free to daily, weekly, monthly, or annual charges. WiFi provides faster Internet access similar to cable and DSL and may be a good tradeoff for those that want higher access speeds and lower costs.

# Kitchen and Dining Area

99. Use the non-slip material. Line your cabinets and drawers with it and it will help muffle noise while driving and keep things in place. It comes in both a thick and a thin version and each works well. Purchase the rolls and cut the specific sizes you need.

100. Flat pot lids are easier to store than taller, dome lids.

A basket is an excellent storage place for your pot and pan lids. This also allows better air circulation if lids are put away when damp.

101. Use lids from copy paper boxes to organize and store canned goods in cabinets. If you don't like the looks of the box, put some decorative paper on it.

Using box lids from paper cartons is a good way to prevent canned goods from shifting around.

102. Always open a refrigerator door and food pantry doors carefully after driving and be prepared to catch falling items. It may be necessary to lay a folded towel on your counter if heavy items tend to fall out.

103. Place egg cartons on shelves lengthwise, front to back—they will never fall out. Use the eggs from the rear of the carton first. This will provide stability when you lift the egg carton.

104. Use some empty egg cartons as separators in your fridge. They will buffer and protect items.

105. Small bungee cords will help stabilize items to your fridge shelves when driving.

106. For a large dish in the fridge (like a leftover casserole), place a piece of the non-slip material over the fridge shelf to keep the dish from sliding.

107. Don't crowd lots of things on the shelf closest to the cooling fins in your refrigerator. Air needs to move over these fins to cool properly.

108. If your fridge has the "Automatic" (AU) setting, this generally means that it will automatically run on electricity when plugged in and on LP gas when not plugged in. You won't have to constantly change it. Also, this setting will protect your food if the park's power (the shore power) goes off.

109. Plastic bins are great for separating dry foods in the cabinets. Use bins with holes in the sides to facilitate air circulation.

Plastic baskets are great for storing dry, lightweight foods.

110. Have some good quality plastic knives, forks, and heavy paper plates (paper, so you can toss them on the campfire, if available) on hand.

111. Store good glassware (like those crystal wine glasses) in the flexible foam drink huggies. Many companies give these away or you can find them at yard sales.

112. If you occasionally need a large pot (such as a Dutch oven), store it outside, underneath.

113. If you occasionally use a pot too large for the kitchen sink—wash it in the bathtub. A plastic tub set into the bathtub works well without filling the bathtub. This also prevents greasy residue in the bathtub.

114. RVs in the medium-priced range may not have any type of flexible sprayer on the kitchen sink. Replacing the faucet with a unit that contains a sprayer built in to the faucet head is an excellent method for solving the sprayer issue.

Perhaps changing faucets will provide more convenience.

115. Sink covers look nice but are nearly useless when preparing food because they eliminate access to the sink. Cutting the larger sink covers in half will allow the cook access to the sink without sacrificing all the surface area. Composite covers can be cut using any

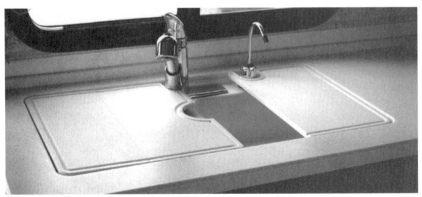
Consider cutting full sink covers to provide more flexibility in their use. Cutting is not detrimental to their look as shown by the cover on the left.

saw with a carbide blade. Use a file to round the edges. After cutting, the four pieces will continue to totally cover the sink if needed.

A second reason for cutting the cover is that this will allow you to place a dish drainer on the edge of the sink and the water will drip in the same sink. Think of this arrangement as access to $1\,^1/_2$ sinks.

Using sink covers that have been cut in two provides greater flexibility in the galley area.

116. The kitchen faucet is easily enhanced by attaching a small, swiveling sprayer. These are inexpensive, available everywhere, and will make your life easier.

117. If you regularly use an electric can opener, store a manual one as a backup.

118. Use a small storage tub tucked back somewhere to hold kitchen gadgets that are occasionally needed but rarely used. Consider this for the grater, knife sharpener, and meat cleaver to name a few.

119. Store bottles of cooking liquids all together in a solid, plastic container when driving. If one happens to break, the spill will be contained. Use an old hand towel to cushion them while driving.

Storing liquids in a solid container will ensure that spills are contained

120. Lay a folded bath towel on top of the turntable in the microwave oven to prevent bouncing while driving.

121. Don't buy in bulk. Whether it is food, laundry supplies, or oil for your car, stop buying in bulk and hauling it around with you. One could argue that what you save on bulk purchases is lost in performance (fuel economy) since you then are forced to haul the extra weight until it is used up.

122. Store bulky kitchen items in a bin.

123. Plan to clean and vacuum more often than you did when living in a house or apartment. Your RV will simply get dirtier faster. This is due to two things. First, the size of the RV forces you to live in a smaller space. For example, you might track dirt into a house but due to the larger space, it is likely scattered. Tracking anything into the RV forces you to use the same door and step into the same area every time. Dirt will accumulate faster.

Store flat cookware (cookie sheets, baking pans, pizza pans) in a wire basket.

Second, living in a house that may be surrounded by grass, trees, and paved streets decreases the potential for blowing dust and dirt. Driving your RV will cause you to be in open spaces more often—such as fueling up or going through construction sites. The potential for blowing dust and dirt to enter your coach is increased with travel.

124. Vacuuming frequently is necessary. Based on the size and year of your coach, you may have a central vacuuming system. Otherwise, a canister vacuum may be easier to manipulate inside the coach. The standard-size upright vacuums typically found in homes may be too unwieldy for some of the confined places in your coach. Finally, don't forget you may have to vacuum the ceilings if the material is "carpet-like"—commonly found in coaches.

# *Bathroom*

125. Inside the medicine cabinet, store the little stuff on the bottom, big stuff on upper shelves to help prevent them from tumbling out.

126. Always open medicine cabinet doors carefully after driving and be prepared to catch falling items. One option, while driving, is to keep a towel in the bathroom sink to cushion the falling items when the medicine cabinet door is first opened.

127. Lay a hand towel on each shelf of the medicine cabinet to cushion the items and prevent them from falling out.

128. There may be some space under your medicine cabinet to install a hanger for drying washcloths. Look for the extra long cabinet handles in your hardware store and use these as hangers.

129. If you need an additional shelf inside the shower, make sure to get one with multiple large suction cups. Thoroughly clean the wall area before you attach the suction cups.

130. Add some permanent towel bars if needed. Think about putting them inside the lavatory, high up near the ceiling.

131. Use towels of different colors for guests traveling with you.

132. To help dry towels, hang them from plastic suit/skirt hangers. These hangers can also be hung from the valance at the top of most slide outs for temporary drying.

133. Put a spring-loaded (tension) curtain rod above the toilet near the ceiling. Multiple suit/skirt hangers can be separated with heavy rubber bands wrapped around the curtain rod.

134. Install a second holder for your shower head. Put this one down low so you can use it to more efficiently rinse if you need to wash a large pot in the bathtub/shower.

135. Use shoeboxes (good sturdy ones with lids) for organizing stuff in the smaller cabinets in the bedroom. Label the ends if necessary.

136. Plastic containers are excellent for storage. You will need some with lids and some without. Use the ones that you can see through. Some RVers prefer the inexpensive wire baskets and shelving to increase the accessibility of drawers and closets.

137. Store your bottles of wine in underwear and sock drawers. Put single bottles in individual paper sacks and then all the individual sacks into one larger one. Lay the large sack on some clothing items and use the rest to pack around the bottles.

# Bedroom and Laundry

138. In some coaches, there is storage under the bed. This is generally accessed by literally lifting the flat platform under the mattress—often from the foot of the bed. This is an excellent place to store extra shoes and items you don't need to frequently access. You may need to use storage boxes. Coach manufacturers are getting better at sealing these areas from outside dust and dirt. If you have a diesel pusher, be careful not to store anything that is sensitive to heat under the bed, since this area can get quite warm.

139. The washer/dryer combination unit found in many larger coaches is a fine machine—but smaller than the one commonly found in the home. Plan to wash and dry smaller loads and expect the clothes to take longer to dry.

140. Heavy items (towels, jeans, sheets) may need to be taken to a regular laundromat.

141. Some RVers do their laundry while driving. The generator will provide power to the washer/dryer. Ensure that you have sufficient fresh water and the

empty grey water tank space when doing this. Some RVers wash several loads while hooked up at the campsite, storing the wet loads in the bathtub, then dry each load while driving. This eliminates the filling of the grey water tank.

142. An "automatic" laundry sorter can be made from canvas bags. These hold just the right amount for one washer load in the combination units. These bags easily unhook and lay on the bed when traveling.

143. When selecting what clothing to bring for living in your coach most of the time (or full time), reduce the number of redundant items.

Use the small canvas-type bags for sorting laundry. These hold one washer-load of clothing—just the right size for the combination washer/dryer units.

# Closets and Storage

144. Use a hook and loop (Velcro®) fastener strap to hold a larger fire extinguisher in the back corner (or corners) of your closet. It's completely out of the way but accessible from the bedroom/bathroom areas.

145. If the longest closet pole is smooth (wood, metal, or plastic), get one of the slip-on coverings for it that contains a series of small ridges. These ridges will help prevent your clothes—on hangers—from sliding to the center while the coach is moving.

    Store a larger fire extinguisher in the back corner of the closet. Use hook-and-loop fastener in the corner.

    Your hanging clothes will tend to slide to the lowest point when driving. This is frequently the cause of the closet pole breaking since all the weight becomes concentrated in one area.

A second method to help distribute this weight is to put your heaviest hanging garments near the two ends of the closet pole where the supports are located.

A third method is to install a closet pole bracket near the middle of the long pole.

Fourth, rotating the pole 180 degrees ($^1/_2$ turn) occasionally will offset the natural bowing that occurs.

146. Purchase one of the small ironing boards with the short folding legs. Store it by attaching it to the back wall of the closet (behind the clothing). Use a hook and loop fastener.

147. Closets often have some type of storage area, accessible from inside the closet and into the right or left wall—an opening that's sometimes literally behind or below a set of drawers, the back of a cabinet, or even a solid panel. This is good storage but hard to get to.

    If you have this type of storage that is an extension of the closet floor, use the plastic tubs with wheels. Put wheels on one end only. You can roll the tub in and out of the storage area easily and when driving, the end without the wheels will prevent it from coming out on its own.

148. The vinyl-clad wire racks and bins are great for storing towels and sheets. They also provide for good air circulation. The ones that stack on one

another can be held together with a cable tie to keep them from bouncing apart while driving.

149. For extra blankets, pillows, sweaters, or any bulky items, use the plastic storage "bags" that have the vacuum attachment in them. Put your items inside the bag, seal it, hook up your vacuum cleaner hose, and suck out the excess air. The bag and contents will seem to collapse to a fraction of the original size. They will expand just fine when you need them.

Driving an RV provides you with the flexibility to travel anywhere such as driving along the Columbia River in Oregon.

# 3 Section

## Outside Stuff While Parked

You must be knowledgeable and prepared to deal with all those things accessible only from the outside and around your RV. Items around your RV must be considered when parked both temporarily and long term. Some of these items are stored in the RV compartments while others belong to the campground.

5th wheels are easy to drive and maneuver.

Most common are the utility hookups at your campsite. Potable (drinkable) water and electricity are commonly found. The most unusual is the sewer connection. The explanation of the sewer system will help you understand how and why to operate this utility.

A new concept in camping—under roof!

Some campsites will have "full hookups"— sites with all three utilities (water, sewer, electricity). Some have water and electricity but no sewer (at the camp site), but there is usually a dump station nearby. Some have water only. Some have no hookups.

Examples of those are the overflow areas of commercial campgrounds, some National and State/Provincial parks, and certainly primitive areas such as BLM (Bureau of Land Management) lands or natural environment/wilderness parks. You should know how to use your RV in these situations—just in case. Experienced RVers often choose limited or no hookups to save camping costs.

Most RVs have outside storage compartments. These are generally spacious cavities accessible through large doors in the side of the RV. Certain doors provide access to your utilities (water, electricity, and sewer). These are not for storage other than the utility connectors (fresh water hose, sewer hose, power cord, and clean-up supplies).

Storage compartments accessible from the outside often hold long-term or bulky items.

Some motorhomes and 5th wheels have storage areas called "pass through." This storage extends from one side of the RV to the other—it passes through the RV. While these pass-through areas are great for storing large amounts of stuff, anything in the middle may be nearly impossible to access easily!

A pass-through storage compartment on a 5th wheel.

A pass-through storage compartment on a motorhome. This rig contains a slide-out tray that makes it easy to access stored items.

An accessory called a "slide tray" is available for the pass-through storage areas. Slide trays are mounted on a roller track that allows you to literally pull out the tray and the stored items some distance. It's like pulling out a drawer—only a drawer with just a bottom and little or no sides.

As with all sections of this book, if the information applies to you, that's great, use it. If the information does not apply to you and your coach, read on.

# Let's Talk About Your Weight

The weight of your RV is important. Weight affects your safety and the safety of others on the road plus the economy and operation of your RV. Weight is also regulated—that is, you must comply with the law wherever you might be driving. While it is impossible to be too underweight, it is dangerous and illegal to be overweight.

5th wheels are popular with the off-road group as you can haul your "toys" in the "toy box" configuration accessible in the rear.

Additionally, all this weight rides on your tires. Therefore, your tires are of the utmost importance since they are the single point of contact between you (or your trailer) and the highway at all speeds. Take good care of your tires.

## *Learning How Much Weight You Can Carry*

All recent RVs must have a label showing the weight capacity of the rig in both empty (unloaded) and maximum weight configurations. This labeling complies with the Recreational Vehicle Industry Association (RVIA) and/or the Federal Government Standards. Locate your label and become familiar with the information. It is often found on the inside of a cabinet or closet and is usually the size of a sheet of paper.

Identifies the actual amount of "stuff" that can be loaded into the coach without exceeding the maximum chassis capacity.

The abbreviations used on the label are fully explained. It is important to recognize that these labels show the estimated **carrying capacity** of this RV. If the RV was manufactured prior to September 2000, the term Net Carrying Capacity (NCC) was used. NCC is the difference between Gross Vehicle Weight Rating (GVWR) and the Unloaded Vehicle Weight (UVW) and **does not** consider the weight of the water, propane, or people you might be carrying. You, the owner, have to remember to factor this in.

In September 2000, the RVIA adopted a new term called Cargo Carrying Capacity (CCC). The CCC is the **difference** between Gross Vehicle Weight Rating (GVWR) **and** the Unloaded Vehicle Weight (UVW) and then subtracts the weight of a full tank of water including water heater, full tank of propane, and the weight of the passengers. The Sleeping Capacity Weight Rating (SCWR) is determined by multiplying 154 pounds (70 kilograms) by the number of sleeping positions. The

The chassis maker's certification of data to the RV manufacturer. This also contains the Vehicle Identification Data.

remaining "unused" weight—the Cargo Carrying Capacity—is the amount of "stuff" you can safely carry before exceeding the manufacturer's Gross Vehicle Weight Rating (GVWR).

The CCC **does not account** for any accessories added to your RV after it was manufactured. The weight of accessories must be deducted from the CCC to determine the actual weight of "stuff" you can pack and take with you. This includes the array of things such as canned goods, clothing, tools, cleaning supplies, dishes, and the coffee pot, to name just a few. Therefore, the CCC directly affects the amount (in weight) of the personal items you can carry.

The total weight of the RV must not exceed its GVWR nor should any axle exceed its particular weight rating. Axles and individual wheel positions can be weighed separately. Each wheel position should not exceed the inflated tire's rated capacity. It has been estimated that over half of all RVs exceed their rated capacity in at least one wheel position.

It is not unusual for one side of an axle to carry more weight than another. For example, if the refrigerator, stove, microwave oven, and sink are all on one side, it is possible that this "kitchen" (or galley, as it is called) side of the coach will weigh more than the opposite side. The RV manufacturer may have compensated for this imbalance by providing more carrying space on the opposite side. Doing so allows you to load more weight on the "under loaded" side. Knowing this implies that the location of what you carry is also important.

Load your RV as you would for normal travel. Locate a public weigh-scale (most commonly found at truck stops). Have your RV and toad, or your tow vehicle and trailer weighed axle-by-axle. The following table will simplify what to weigh and why.

Common at truck stops, a certified scale will handle any size RV.

## What and Why to Weigh

|  | Motorhome | Towed Vehicle (Toad) | Truck/Car for Pulling | Trailer or 5th Wheel |
|---|---|---|---|---|
| What To Weigh | Total weight. First, all axles on scale. Second, each axle separately. | Total weight. First, all axles on scale. Second, each axle separately. | Total weight. First, all axles on scale. Second, each axle separately. | Total weight. First, all axles on scale. Second, each axle separately. |
| Why Weigh This | Cannot exceed the GVWR, axle weight ratings (FAWR, RAWR) or the tire ratings. | Prevent overloading the toad or exceeding hitch/towing capacity. | Prevent overloading the vehicle, its rear axle(s), or underweighting the front axle. | Cannot exceed the GVWR, axle weight ratings, or the tire ratings. nor the tow vehicle's capacity. |
| Safety Is Compromised! | It is unlawful and affects safety and handling. | The hitch, suspension, tow bar, and tires may exceed their rated capacity. | May exceed Gross Combined Weight Rating (GCWR) or the towing capacity of the vehicle. | It is unlawful and affects safety and handling. The hitch, trailer suspension, and tires may exceed their rated capacity. |

Ideally, it is best to have it weighed wheel by wheel, to determine how much remaining capacity you may have, and where it is located. This process will verify if you need to rearrange what you are carrying to better balance the RV.

However, locating facilities to weigh each wheel position is more difficult. Sometimes you can move slightly off the truck scale in such a way that you can obtain individual wheel weights. Often, this service is provided at RV rallies and shows and the weighing may be part of a safety seminar. There are private companies providing weighing services at these events and in campgrounds as well. All will physically weigh your coach or trailer by individual wheel position.

Once you know the weight on each tire position, you can easily determine if you exceed any specification—tire, axle, or vehicle—and make adjustments accordingly.

## *Learning About Weight and Your RV Tires*

RV manufacturers must certify the tires and tire pressures required to support the vehicle. On drivable RVs, there will be a Federal (or Canadian) Motor Vehicle Safety Standards (FMVSS / CMVSS) compliance label (data plate) in the area of the driver's seat. (The label shows the Gross Vehicle Weight Rating (GVWR), the individual Gross Axle Weight Ratings (GAWR), and the Gross Combined Weight Rating (GCWR) that was determined by the final body-builder or

This US label certifies the vehicle meets applicable safety standards, tire and rim sizes, and tire pressures required to comply.

manufacturer. The manufacturer will certify the capacity of the vehicle as it was built with the tires and tire pressures required to support this capacity and this will be shown on the label.

Tires on motorhomes are "truck" tires although many are specially manufactured for RVs. The RV tires often have high weight-carrying capacities and a UV protectant in the rubber. Ratings marked on their sidewalls show the maximum carrying capacity based on a maximum tire pressure for both single- and dual-wheel configurations. If you should lower the air pressure, you will reduce the capacity of the tire and the amount of load-carrying capacity of the RV.

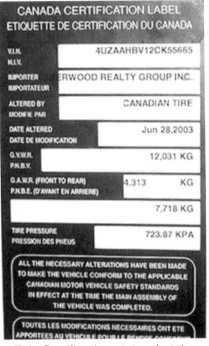

| CANADA CERTIFICATION LABEL | |
| --- | --- |
| ÉTIQUETTE DE CERTIFICATION DU CANADA | |
| V.I.N. N.I.V. | 4UZAAHBV12CK55665 |
| IMPORTER IMPORTATEUR | ERWOOD REALTY GROUP INC. |
| ALTERED BY MODIFIE PAR | CANADIAN TIRE |
| DATE ALTERED DATE DE MODIFICATION | Jun 28, 2003 |
| G.V.W.R. P.N.B.V. | 12,031 KG |
| G.A.W.R. (FRONT TO REAR) P.N.B.E. (D'AVANT EN ARRIERE) | 4,313 KG |
| | 7,718 KG |
| TIRE PRESSURE PRESSION DES PNEUS | 723.87 KPA |

ALL THE NECESSARY ALTERATIONS HAVE BEEN MADE TO MAKE THE VEHICLE CONFORM TO THE APPLICABLE CANADIAN MOTOR VEHICLE SAFETY STANDARDS IN EFFECT AT THE TIME THE MAIN ASSEMBLY OF THE VEHICLE WAS COMPLETED.

TOUTES LES MODIFICATIONS NECESSAIRES ONT ETE APPORTEES AU VEHICULE POUR LE RENDRE CONFORME

This Certification states that the vehicle has been inspected and meets the Canadian Motor Vehicle Safety Standards. It contains information similar to the US label. All measurements are metric.

You should contact the tire manufacturer and obtain the tire load charts or booklet that specifies the weight carrying capacity for your tires at various tire pressures. It is strongly recommended that you do this. Their information will also include how to properly check your tire pressure (always when cold), how to safely add air (remember, 105 pounds of pressure in a tire casing is **high pressure** and deadly if the tire blows), and how to determine how old the tire is (the DOT Code).

Always keep the same pressure on each side of an axle. Determine this specified pressure by using the tire pressure required to support the weight on the most heavily loaded wheel position.

Always keep the same pressure on each side of an axle

You may hear talk among RVers about adding some extra air for safety. Tire manufacturers **used** to recommend increasing the tire pressure by ten percent (10%) above the amount required to carry the load you determined by the weighing process. Theoretically, this provided a margin of safety and allowed for the natural depletion of air pressure as time passed. However, that 10% recommendation is now built into the tire ratings for the RV type tires. There's no need to add more.

One of the major factors in tire wear and failure is under inflation. It is imperative that you know the weight of your RV and how much air to put in your tires. Therefore, to be safe, comply with the laws, and save money, know your RV weight and tire pressure. Load your RV carefully and knowledgeably. Plus, make sure to **frequently** check your tire pressure when cold at the start of each day. Use a good quality, accurate tire pressure gauge.

# Packing Your RV

150. The "Packing Rule" is... Light stuff high and forward, heavy stuff low and back.

151. Balance the load side-to-side.

152. Use big plastic containers to organize stuff in the outside compartments.

153. Check your LP gas and fill the tank if needed since it may be difficult to find an LP dealer on the road. Using their respective power switches, you must shut off all gas appliances while filling. There may be a master shut-off switch on your RV tanks. This master switch does not turn on the appliances—only the LP. Don't forget to turn this back on before driving away.

Getting propane is one of the normal tasks. You usually have to have everyone and all pets out of the coach before fueling can begin. Plus, all propane appliances must be shut off— that is, no open flames.

154. If you carry a gas grill and have a standard-size, portable LP gas tank, this size of tank will fit perfectly into the "milk crate" type container.

An alternative is to use the LP gas already onboard and place a quick disconnect hose connection in the line near the tank. You can connect your gas grill to this connection by means of a rated gas hose. This provides an extra measure of safety and eliminates the space required to carry the extra tank.

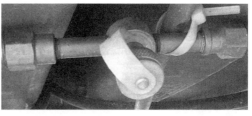

Shows an accessory connection to the LP system that allows the RVer to safely use propane from the RV LP tank. This accessory eliminates the need to carry portable LP bottles.

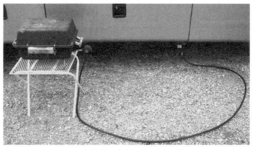

An accessory kit that includes the propane tank connector, a suitable gas rated LP hose, and a connector for the LP grill.

155. If you have pass-through storage, long items are no problem. Coaches without pass-through storage often have open space inside and across the top of several individual compartments. You may be able to use this space for extra long items.

Walls separating compartments may not reach the top

# When You First Pull Into the Campsite

156. Just prior to pulling (or backing) in, the copilot should go outside and do a quick scan of the site. You do not want to run over or into anything that may have been left by the previous occupant. Check

Here is a shallow campsite in a state park. You will need to discuss your length needs when you register or when you call to reserve a site.

the picnic table. Is it too close to where the coach needs to be? Remember: You generally drive straight out of a site but nearly always have to turn to drive or back in. You could, for example, drive out of a site with the picnic table nearly touching the coach but likely cannot drive or backup into the same site without moving it.

157. With the copilot's guidance, position the coach on the site.

158. You may need to take a quick measure before putting the slides out. Look for obstacles (tree limbs, shore power poles, picnic tables, etc.) that the slide could hit. A handy "tool" with which to measure your slide clearance is the metal "hook" used for grabbing the awning loop. Put pieces of tape or use a permanent marker on the metal hook to indicate the necessary clearance for the slides.

This coach was positioned too close to the power panel. Serious slide damage was apparently avoided by luck!

159. Dump the air from the air bags. Your bottom step will be closer to the ground and your jacks won't have to extend as far.

It's okay to leave your toad connected when you dump the air from the air bags on a drive-through site. **Always disconnect the toad before backing up into a campsite**.

160. Level the coach. Follow the coach manufacturer's instructions as to what sequence to use. An improper sequence may, in fact, cause the coach to actually

twist and possibly cause damage. The rule-of-thumb is to first level what is called "north and south." (North and south" is RV jargon for front-to-back, or referring to lengthwise on the coach.) Then, when close, level sideways.

The coach does not have to be perfectly level, close is okay. Some RVers prefer theirs to be slightly unlevel to ensure that the water in the tub/shower will flow to the drain, i.e., no standing water in the back or sides of the tub.

There are various means to determine level in your coach or trailer...

- Use a large trailer level mounted on the front and visible from the jack controls on the trailer, together with a side mounted level to judge the north-south level.

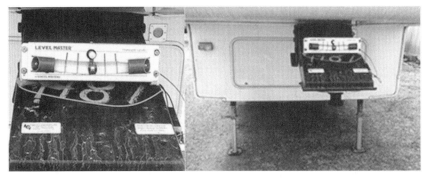

A large level that allows the RVer to easily see that the trailer is level from the towing vehicle (regular and close-up view shown). A side mounted level allows front to rear leveling when standing at the leveling-jack control center.

- Use the round bubble level that manufacturers sometimes install inside the coach. Before attempting to use this level for the first time, determine whether it has been leveled with the coach. First, level the coach by placing an 18″

(0.5 m) level on the bottom floor of the refrigerator. Once level lengthwise (north/south) adjust the screws on the bottom of the level to center the bubble.

Repeat this process for the east/west (sideways). You can now trust the bubble level to accurately indicate if the coach is level or not. These can be tricky to judge. It takes practice.

• Use a set of levels—one small level is usually attached to the sidewall for front-to-back leveling. The second small level is likely attached to the dash for side-to-side leveling. These are pretty easy to use and allow the driver to level the coach without help.

• Ask the copilot to place a refrigerator level on a shelf in the refrigerator and have them confirm when the coach is level.

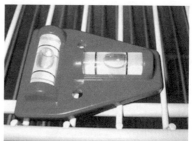

A "two-way" level (one you do not have to reposition) will give you accurate readings when placed on the shelf in the refrigerator.

• Use a small can of tomato paste, which is thick and will not move inside the can itself. Lay it on your kitchen counter. If it rolls, adjust the jacks accordingly.

161. If there is an unlevel or inclined parking space, try using one or two boards under the jacks that have to move the farthest. Be careful when adding boards since you do not want to raise any tire off the ground. The wheels should carry the weight and the jack should stabilize the body.

162. Slides go out after leveling. Some manufacturers may recommend that you start the engine to provide maximum power to the electric motors that operate the slides. This is true for putting the slides out and in. As previously noted, some manufacturers may require the engine to be shut off before the slides can be moved. Check your manual.

Dual slides on the driver side of a motorhome are shown in the "out" position.

# Hooking Up the Coach at the Campsite

## Overview...

Share the inside and outside work with the copilot, if possible. Whether you are entering a pull-through (becoming more common as campgrounds are updated) or a back-in site, you will need some communication. Use the hand-held (also called an FRS or two-way) radios for general communication and certainly, hand signals while backing into a site.

Always use someone outside the RV to help guide you when backing.

Note: As a safety precaution, the copilot should never stand behind the coach when it is backing up. Always have the copilot visible in the driver's side mirror.

One example of sharing would be as follows…

The copilot is outside guiding you into the site (sometimes with the help of the campground personnel). Finally, you stop. The copilot does a quick walk-around to make sure everything is clear and lets you know.

**Inside (Immediately)**… With the engine running, dump your air bags, start the jacks going down (about halfway). If needed, the copilot will use the metal awning hook to guide some boards under your jacks. The copilot will let you know. Finish putting down the jacks and get it level.

Put out the slides. When the slides are out, shut off the engine and go outside to help.

- Total time for leveling and slides is about 5–6 minutes with practice.

**Outside (As soon as the jacks are down)**… Get the power cord out of the coach. **Check the campsite's shore power breaker and turn it off!** Confirm that the post power is correctly wired with a simple plug-in tester. If all is okay, plug in. (See below for correct sequence)

Potable water hose is next. Run the faucet a bit and connect the hose to both the faucet and coach inlet.

Sewer hose is last. Do you really need to hook this up? … for just one night? If so, hook the coach end first and then stretch the hose to the park's sewer connection. Double-check your connections.

Leave the grey water valve closed to allow grey water to build up. You will use the grey water in this tank to flush out the dump hose after dumping your black water tank. If you do not need to dump black water, open the grey water valve only. Leave this open all the time while parked.

If you **need to dump black water**, see "Sewer Connection—Operation or How to Dump" for additional information and suggestions.

• Total time is about 8–10 minutes with practice.

163. Turn the circuit breaker switch **off** at the shore power before plugging in!

Just for fun, note the times that you pull into a campsite and the breaker is still on. That tells you that the previous occupant is living dangerously!

164. Electricity first, potable water second, sewage third, wash hands fourth.

Turn the circuit breaker switch **off** at the shore power before plugging in! Turn it back on after plugging in.

• Electricity first because your hands are dry.

• Potable water (your water hose) second because you haven't handled the sewer hose yet so you won't contaminate the good water supply.

• Sewer hose is last and then try to not touch anything until you can wash thoroughly.

• Wash hands immediately and thoroughly. A germicidal soap is best.

165. Standard rule for water hose color is white for potable water and green for everything else. This is changing and some hoses are now available in "designer" colors. Get a new hose for potable water with any rig and that way you will know it is clean.

A power reel is available for your water hose and can be added to most any RV.

166. Make certain you have purchased a water-pressure regulator for your potable water hose. This regulator will prevent excessively high water pressure from entering your coach. Some campgrounds have very high water pressure. You may see signs at the campground office warning of this high pressure and, if so, take them seriously to prevent damage to your coach. It is best to always use the regulator. Make it a (mostly) permanent attachment.

Attach the water pressure regulator between the campsite supply and your hose. This will prevent any high pressure from blowing out your water hose.

Attach the water pressure regulator to the end of your water hose that attaches to the campground faucet. Doing this will prevent high water pressure from bursting your water hose—since the pressure is regulated at the faucet.

167. Before attaching the water hose, run the water for a few seconds at high pressure just to wash off the faucet end and ensure no critters are up, inside the end of the faucet.

168. Some people spray a disinfectant onto the end of the faucet and give it a few seconds to work on any residual bacteria.

169. Buy an old pair of channel-lock pliers at a yard sale and keep them in the water compartment for tightening the hose and you won't have to remember to take them with you every time. They will rust, so an occasional bit of lubricant helps.

170. Using a "quick disconnect" for your potable water hose connections make this task easy.

171. Keep a box of the disposable rubber gloves in the outside water compartment. Use them if you get into raw sewage. They can be purchased at any pharmacy. Don't save and reuse the gloves. Toss them when you are finished.

A "quick release" connector makes connecting the water hose quick and easy.

172. Use a mat on the outside ground so shoes can be wiped before coming into the coach. Store the mat on the inside bottom step when driving.

173. If you manually crank up your TV antenna or satellite dish, hang your coach keys from the crank. That way, you won't drive away without remembering to lower these items. Don't delay or you will forget. The best way is to have the keys in hand when you crank.

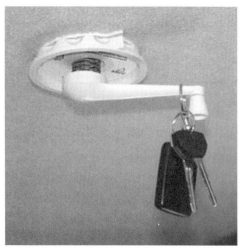

Hanging your RV ignition keys from your TV antenna (or satellite dish crank) will help ensure you will lower it before driving away.

Another method is to use a twist-tie. Fasten it to the antenna crank while the antenna is down (stowed) so it will be handy. Fasten it to the steering wheel while the antenna is up.

Still another method is to use a "red flag." There is one available that says "Remove Before Flight," and it's used on aircraft to remind you to take off the control locks, gear locking pins, etc. Tie it to the antenna crank while the antenna is down (stowed) and move it to the steering wheel while the antenna is up.

174. If the wind is gusting, don't put out your awning. If the wind picks up later, store the awning. Some RVers use a tie down kit to avoid damage to the awning if a wind suddenly comes up. These kits are quite effective in moderate winds but storing the awning is always best and safest in windy situations.

175. Lay sun shades (may be called sun screens) out in the sun for a few minutes, or bring them inside (in cooler/colder weather), before attempting to attach them to the coach. Use a

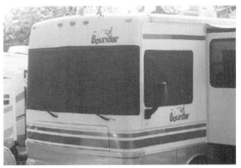
Black sun screens attached to a coach.

picnic table or the hood or roof of the car to lay them out. Some types need to be stretched a bit to fasten and they stretch easier when warmed up. If you need to stretch your shades a bit (to reach the fastener), you can pull on the material but not the edging.

176. When putting up your awning, leave one end slightly lower than the other. This will allow water to run off and be directed to the back or front of the awning—away from the coach door.

Tilting an awning slightly will divert water away from your door, walkway, or table.

177. If the wind is really gusting, don't put up your TV antenna and satellite dish. They could become damaged or bend in the high winds.

The "batwing" antenna is designed to lay on the roof of the RV and not be affected by high winds when driving.

178. A campground may advertise "instant" phone sites. These are ones that allow you to attach a standard phone cable between your coach and the campground phone plug located near the shore power box. This provides instant access to the phone—and typically local calls are free. The "800" number calls are, of course, free. You cannot make long distance calls from the instant phone sites unless you have a pre-paid card or have made arrangements for the charges.

Don't forget to carry a length of phone cord and a "normal" telephone.

# Checking Shore Power

The term "shore power" was derived from the electrical connections that boats plug into in a marina. The receptacle (electrical power) was literally "on shore." RVers adopted that jargon. Therefore, shore power is the (usually) grey box containing electrical power located at respective campsites.

There are three items that must be considered when connecting to shore power at any location. They are:

A typical shore power stand and panel found is many campgrounds. Most have 50-amp, 30-amp, and 20 amp receptacles available.

- The power supply has the capacity you require.

- Whether the receptacles are correctly wired and are safe to use.

- The level of voltage available.

**Ensure that the supply has the capacity you require**...
Look at the circuit breaker controlling the outlet. It may
be marked with 15, 20, 30, or 50 amps. That will be the
maximum rating of the circuit.

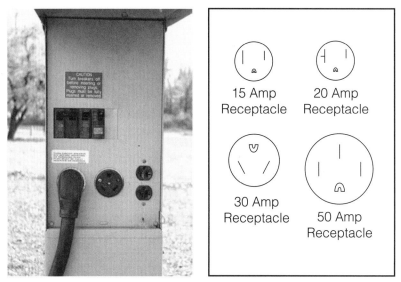

Shore power receptacles in 15, 20, 30-amp, and 50-amp
configurations. You can visually determine what type of
campground service is available if there is no local circuit breaker. If
possible, confirm the size of service by looking for the amp rating
stamped on the breaker handle.

The 15- and 20-amp receptacles are commonly found in
older campgrounds and smaller state or provincial parks.
These receptacles look like the standard ones found in
your home. The 30- and 50-amp power sources have their
own special receptacle and you may be able to plug your
power cord directly into the appropriate one. In some
cases, you will need an adapter. If so, choose the
"dogbone" style that separates the ends to allow heat to
dissipate. Some campgrounds have added the 30-amp
receptacles but have not upgraded their wiring, so the
circuit breaker marking will tell you the circuit capacity.

**Determine that the receptacles are correctly wired and are safe to use**... This is becoming a critical issue, with all the electronic equipment found in modern RVs. Test the shore power before plugging in.

This device is designed to check the status of the wiring in the shore power panel. It will warn you if the wiring is incorrect.

Buy and always use a plug-in circuit tester that uses colored lights to confirm okay or indicate various faults.

Occasionally, you will need adapters to use the receptacle. You can also use adapters to test the socket you are actually going to

A device to determine if the shore power circuits are properly wired and have all wire connections present. Use this before connecting the RV to the power source. (Shown inside for clarity)

plug your shore power cord into. Plug in the adapter, turn on the circuit breaker, and confirm the condition.

**What is the level of voltage available...** You should not use your air conditioners if the incoming power is less than 105 volts. A simple test meter will help confirm the correct voltage at the campground supply when you are connecting to it. If the voltage is high enough, with the breaker turned off, connect your power cord. Then turn on the breaker.

A typical digital readout meter that shows AC line voltage and measures DC (battery) power, resistance, and light current draws. (Shown being used inside for clarity)

Many RVers use surge protection devices. There are portable ones that may be connected to the campground's shore power supply or others hardwired inside the RV at the power cord entry point. The more sophisticated models protect against damaging power surges and shut down the power if the voltage drops too low or spikes to an unsafe level. They also have built-in delay circuits to protect air conditioning compressors when they restart after a power change. Surge protection devices may not operate if connected to a power source with unsafe wiring. Some models provide a read-out of the problem, provide a display of operations, and have an override function in the event of a component failure. Using these sophisticated systems makes some of the campsite checking redundant.

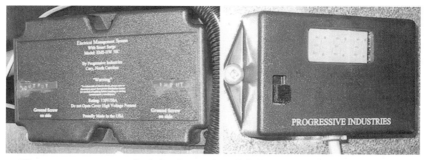

These systems monitor the incoming AC line power and shunt high surges to ground providing protection for the RV systems. Many also monitor the line voltage, amperage or watts being consumed, line frequency and whether there have been any aberrations in these monitored conditions. System shown is "hard-wired" (or permanently installed) and includes a Remote Display panel. Other versions are portable for connecting to the shore cord at the power source.

A plug-in device suitable for monitoring AC line voltage during the time the RV is connected to any source of AC power.

The last electric monitor that all RVers should consider is a line voltage monitor. This monitor should be placed in a highly visible location (often in the kitchen) and regularly checked to see if the voltage has risen or fallen into unsafe ranges. The analog styles usually have a color-coded scale and are okay if in the green and not okay if in the red.

Voltage can change. For example, if you plugged into a campground source early on a hot summer day, you may have received an acceptable voltage reading. However, as the day warms up and more RVers turn on their air conditioners, the campground's power supply may not be able to keep the voltage high enough to avoid damage to your air conditioner compressors. If you regularly check your monitor, you will know if the voltage is in an unsafe range and can turn off the air conditioners until the voltage rises again. You may also reduce your electrical usage by allowing your refrigerator to switch over to LP gas and even turning off the charger or converter.

It is recommended that you turn off your generator before connecting to the shore power. Most RVs have a power transfer switch designed to automatically switch from the generator input. Switching off your generator prior to connecting is good practice.

Good electrical-power-connection practice is to put one hand in your pocket and make the connection with the other hand. This avoids a possible short circuit path across your chest (heart) in event of a wiring problem.

Note: Some of the devices shown in this chapter are available at hardware outlets. They may also be available at camping and RV dealers.

# Sewer Connections

## Overview...

The RV's sewer connection is probably the most unfamiliar apparatus on the coach that you have to physically operate. Every other appliance has a counterpart in the home and yes, while homes have a sewer system, they are, for the most part, hidden. They work and you rarely have to deal with them.

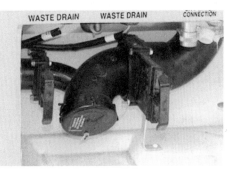

The sewer connection at the RV. Two blade valves are shown. Black water is on the right and is a larger pipe. Grey water is left and may be a smaller pipe.

Therefore, an overview, or explanation is offered here since you have to be able to operate your sewer on a regular and frequent basis. Even if your coach is parked for a long period of time and you are living in it, you will have to operate the sewer—it is not automatic.

Our purpose is not to be crude but to explain as clearly as possible how to deal with this necessity when living in your coach.

# Non-technical Explanation...

There are two "holding tanks" on modern coaches. One is called "grey water" and is designed to hold the runoff from all sinks and the shower. The second is called the "black water" and is designed to hold the sewage resulting from flushing the toilet. The two tanks are not connected except at the drain connection.

Both tanks are usually drained using controls on the outside. Each tank has a shutoff, called a "blade valve," typically accessible in the utility compartment. When you open (pull out) the respective blade valve, either the black water or grey water is directed (flows) into a single, large pipe. Connect your sewer hose to the end of this pipe. There is a cap for this pipe and you should use it when driving. It will prevent any drips from landing on the bottom of your compartment.

The sewer connection at the RV. The two blade valves are shown. This time, the black water is on the left and grey water is on the right. Always carefully check.

The infamous sewer hose "hump" ensures a blockage. The hose will fill without flowing.

Sewer hoses are approximately 3-inch-diameter flexible hose. There must be a connector fastened to one end. That connector will attach and lock onto the end of the pipe in the coach.

The other end of the sewer hose must go into the sewer access, usually some type of pipe or, at minimum, a hole in the ground, at your campsite or dump station. There are several universal-type adapters you can use for this connection.

It is highly recommended that you use a connector rather than just sticking the end of your flexible sewer hose in the sewer access hole. A connector will form somewhat of a seal that helps prevent both odors and splash back. Also available, is a rubber "collar" (adaptor ring—the donut) that fits around the connection to help the seal. It is common to have and use both when needed. Some places require the use of the rubber adaptor ring (donut).

A common arrangement is to have the right-angle attachment used to connect the sewer hose to the ground connection. This also shows a rubber collar (sometimes called a "donut") that forms a seal between the ground connection and the end of the hose apparatus. Many areas require the use of donuts.

# What You Need...

Sewer hoses are commonly available in lengths of 10 feet or 20 feet. There are also connectors that allow you to hook two hoses together for extra length. Carry at least 20 feet of hose because sometimes you just can't park close enough to connect.

There are plastic and aluminum "racks" that expand to fit underneath your sewer hose and allow it to drain down an incline. These are often helpful and useful in many situations. There will be times when you cannot use these or using them would have no effect on the drainage.

You can purchase an apparatus that holds the sewer hose and forces it to follow an incline.

# Operation or How to Dump...

When stopping at a campsite for the night or if you find a dump station, position the coach 5–10 feet away from the ground access. Parking too close will often force the hose to form into tight curves and hamper the flow. Attach the sewer hose connector to the end of the discharge pipe in or near your utility compartment and **lock it in place**. Place the other end in the ground access. Then, arrange your sewer hose so that it is the straightest possible run from one connection to the other. A second option is to expand the hose to form a wide gentle curve. You do not want tight twists and turns in the hose that would slow down or hinder the flow of sewage running through the sewer hose.

A prize-winning sewer hose display. This particular hose configuration will force all residue to actually climb two hills before reaching the ground connection. This is definitely a "how-not-to."

Another sewer "how-not-to." The tight curves in the hose will literally stop solids from moving while water flows past.

Campsites normally have a rock or brick next to the sewer. Use this to hold down the sewer hose. Some people hold it down with their foot but if any splashing occurs, you will carry the sewage back into the coach.

RVers often carry a brick, rock, or heavy board to help hold down the end of the sewer hose.

Dump the **black water first**! Pull open the **black water** blade valve. When finished, close the valve. If your RV has a black water flushing system then connect a hose (do not use your potable water hose!) to the fitting, preferably through an anti-siphon valve. Turn on the hose and allow it to run for two or three minutes to flush the black tank, and clean off the tank sensors, then turn off the water. Re-open the black tank blade valve and drain the water and remaining material once again.

An anti-siphon valve prevents anything in the flushing line from flowing back into the hose that is connected to a water source.

It is recommended that you use a clear fitting at the connection between the dump hose and the tanks to allow you to monitor the progress of the flushing process. Repeat this procedure until the water flowing out is clear. Then close the valve and turn on the water hose for another two or three minutes. This will put some water in the tank that will slosh around and loosen any dried material in the tank, so that it can be drained next time.

Clear adapters allow you to visually monitor the effluent (sewage) as it is dumped to help determine when the waste tank is clean.

Various clear adapters are available to help you monitor the dumping process.

Next, open the grey water blade valve and dump the grey water. Dumping in this sequence will allow the soapy grey water, (runoff from the sinks and shower) to literally wash out the sewer hose. This will ensure that residue in the hose from the black water tank will be washed away.

After dumping your black water, add the toilet chemical (preferably those which are bio-degradable and do not contain any formaldehyde). Read the toilet chemical package and follow specific directions. It's best to run 2–3 gallons of fresh water into the tank by holding the flush lever open or adding as mentioned above. Don't skimp on this initial water by convincing yourself that if you use just a little, you won't have to dump as often. The black water tank must have a liquid base to ensure efficient breakdown of solids, and proper dumping of all material.

You must use toilet chemicals to help the operation of the sewage system. Toilet chemicals help prevent problems. The three primary black water tank problems are deodorizing, cleaning, and the breakdown of solid waste.

There are numerous brands available and they come in liquid, tablet, powder, or "tab" (a small, self-contained packet that is just dropped in, whole). Some RVers mix their own. But everyone uses toilet chemicals. Plan for it.

## When to Dump...

Dump your black water when the tank is approximately $1/2$ to $3/4$ full. If two adults are traveling in a coach, it may be several days before you need to dump the black water.

You also need about a half-tank of grey water to effectively flush out the sewer hose after dumping the black water. Many RVers actually camp with both tanks closed.

Then at some point, they dump. You can periodically dump some of the grey water.

The best time to dump is after a lengthy drive and as soon as you hook up. The driving will cause the residue in the black water tank to jostle and mix and help break up the solids. This liquid mixture will drain efficiently.

**Never leave your black water valve open all the time—** even when camping long term! The solids in the black water tank will not flow down the sewer hose. These solids need to be "broken down" inside the black water tank in order to flow out efficiently.

Here's why. If the coach is not moving (parked for a few days), the black water tank actually functions like an old "outhouse" or portable toilet. Solids will stack and form what some RVers refer to as the "cone of crap." While there is water in the tank as a result of the flushing, there is no physical movement to "stir it up" or mix the liquid and solids. That's why it is best to dump the black water right after a drive.

## Safety and Cleanliness...

You will be working with raw sewage and you will get it on you. You can try the disposable rubber gloves but they will easily tear. Some people use the heavy, large rubber gloves. They work but you must still wash them to reduce bacteria. Most people simply use their bare hands and with practice, there is virtually no splash or spillage.

Without question, the most difficult part of the whole sewage process is storing the sewer hose when getting ready to travel. It is drippy. It sometimes smells. It sometimes has residue on it. Some RVers try to store it in a garbage bag but it will not dry out during the day. Most just coil it up and stuff the hose into the sewage compartment.

Some coaches have a built-in black water tank "flush" system. If you can see the end of your black water tank then these fittings can simply be added to your tank. This is a method of cleaning the inside of the black water tank and should be done periodically. The flush system is made up of permanently mounted spray nozzles, inside the black water tank. You must hook up a garden hose to connect these nozzles to a faucet, turn on the water, and let it spray for a few minutes. Supposedly, residual solids and paper are washed off the tank walls and sensors. You may have to spray the flush system several times to achieve the best results. These flush systems do okay and help, but they are not perfect.

**Do not** use your potable water hose to flush your black water tank. Use a readily available anti-siphon valve since there is a remote chance of getting some backflow into the hose. You really don't want

An aftermarket black water tank flushing fitting designed to be mounted on the black water tank. A hose can be connected during tank draining to flush out effluent and clean off tank monitor sensors.

A flushing hose connection that allows any backflow from the anti-siphon valve to drain outside the RV.

that to happen! Carry a second hose to use for everything except drinking water!

Since the RV toilet functions like the outhouse, you can do away with the toilet plunger. There is no use for one in your RV. While there are several models of toilets, one of the most common uses a moveable valve, located at the bottom of the bowl, for flushing. To flush, step on the lever at the side of the toilet bowl. This causes the valve to open, flush water to start flowing, and the resulting residue to drop into the black water tank. When you release the lever, the valve closes and seats into a groove. This seals the bottom of the toilet bowl and allows water to remain in the bowl between uses.

A marine-type toilet is common in most RVs There is usually a foot pedal for flushing. You push it down for flushing and raise it up to add water to the bowl. The ball valve shown in the bottom of the bowl must be kept clean of residue. Otherwise, it will not seal, allowing water to drain away and odors to enter the coach.

While this is nearly a foolproof system, any residue lodged within the actual valve will prevent it from seating correctly. This will result in water leaking into the black water tank and allow odors to enter the coach. If necessary, soft residue **must** be cleaned from the valve immediately,. Use a standard toilet brush for cleaning this valve.

179. Your coach should have grey and black water level indicator lights. These give you a fair reading of the volume in the respective tanks.

180. Indicator lights on the black water tank are driven by sensors inside the tank. If something is caught on the sensor (like toilet paper), the indicator light will come on and you will get a false reading.

181. If you overfill the grey water, it will simply back up into the bathtub (or shower drain) as it is the lowest drain in the coach. There will be some odor but this will go away when you dump.

182. RV toilet manufacturers recommend using toilet paper specially manufactured for RVs as this breaks down easier. Many RVers use the residential-type single-ply tissue since it is less expensive.

183. The rule-of-thumb is that when the coach sits for a long period of time (the sewage is not jostled and mixed from driving), use the RV-type since the breakdown of the tissue is based on the effectiveness of the toilet chemical. If you are driving frequently, the residential-type tissue will break down from both the movement and the toilet chemical.

184. Add toilet chemicals after dumping the black water.

185. Use the black water tank flush preferably each time you dump, otherwise periodically. This is simply good, and easy, maintenance.

186. A serious grey or black tank cleaning can be done in two ways.

   • Fill the tank, almost full, with hot water. This is impossible with the on-board water heater so you must be able to connect a hose to a large residential-size water heater to do this. Drive around. The hot water will slosh around to loosen and clean residue.

- Another method is to add about 15–20 pounds (couple of big bags) of ice cubes (not crushed ice but actual cubes) through the toilet. Then add 5–10 gallons of water and drive around. The ice cubes will literally abrade remaining residue. When the ice melts, you can drain the tank normally.

# Unhooking—Getting Ready to Go

187. Turn off all electric items in the RV then turn the breaker switch **off** at the shore power before unplugging!

188. Remember: Electricity first, potable water second, sewage third, hand-washing fourth.

189. Electric is first—because your hands are dry. Potable water (your water hose) is second—because you haven't handled the sewer hose yet, so you won't contaminate the

The electrical compartment houses and protects the inverter and the coiled electric cord.

good water supply. Sewer hose is last—and then try to not touch anything until you can wash thoroughly.

190. Both the 50-amp and 30-amp plugs are large and sometimes difficult to pull apart and/or pull out. Generally, you tend to try to wrap your fingers

around the end just to get a better grasp of the male end—especially when trying to unplug from a shore power box. A flat band affixed to the male end will provide a loop into which you can insert your hand for easier pulling.

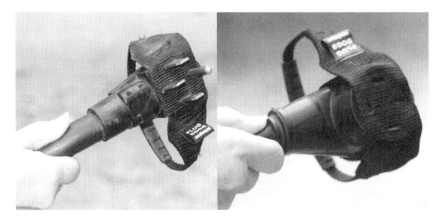

This apparatus on the left is fastened over the plugs for ease in pulling them apart. A matching apparatus shown on the right fits over a female plug. Shown here is the 50-amp receiver end on a 30-amp adapter.

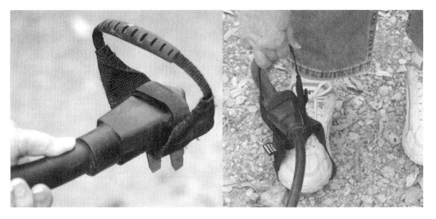

The loop will make it easier to grasp the plug ends to pull them apart. The loops also provide more holding power for pulling. As shown here, use your foot!

191. Disconnect your hose, drain it, and connect the two ends of your water hose to each other to prevent anything from getting inside the hose while traveling.

A couple of times a year, it is advisable to add two or three tablespoons of bleach to a partially full hose, almost fill it and then connect the ends together. At the next stop connect the hose and flush out the bleach solution and connect as usual. Some RVers use quick disconnects and a two-way diverter valve to allow them to relieve the water pressure from the RV hose before disconnecting the line.

The water compartment houses and protects all water hookups.

A simple Y-adapter with shut off valves that allow water to be obtained when connected to a hose bib. It also allows the pressure to be relieved from the RV connection before releasing the hose. Doing this prevents you from being sprayed with water still under pressure. Turn off the hose bib tap, open the short hose shutoff valve, and the pressurized water will flow from the RV hose to the short hose. Remove RV hose and store. Note the pressure regulator is mounted before the shut-off Y for protection of the hose.

192. If your sewer hose dripped while unhooking, wash up the ground area.

193. Don't forget to pick up any boards you put under your jacks. Sometimes these are actually pushed into the ground. If so, dig them out. Use your awning hook to grab them.

194. Lower your TV antenna and satellite dish. If you are not sure if they are up, check by cranking up a few turns and then back down again. You cannot tell by simply looking at the crank!

195. Check your entry steps. Make sure they are retracted, and store any doormats you may have used.

196. If you have sun shades (sun screens) remove them and roll them—don't fold them—for storage.

197. Extend your main and window awnings according to the manufacturer's instructions. If the large, main awning is a manual one, the roller is under a great deal of spring tension. First, ensure that no one will open the door while you are extending the awning or you run the risk of ripping the awning fabric with the corner of the door. Extend the awning to the lowest setting on each end. Loosen the upper arm thumbscrews and release the ends near the roller. Slide the upper arms down toward the coach body.

Grasp the nylon strap and slide it toward the front where the awning lock lever is located. With firm pressure on the strap, use your awning rod to unlock the lever. Pulling firmly on the strap, slide the strap across to the middle of the awning, then carefully and slowly reduce pressure on the strap and guide it as the spring pressure on the roller pulls the awning up toward the body to its stored position. For the last few feet you will need the awning rod to hold and guide the strap. Once the awning is fully retracted, ensure that it is locked if you have a locking mechanism, then tighten all thumbscrews on the support rods.

If your awning supports tend to rattle a bit while driving, put an old deflated tennis ball between the support and the coach wall. This will stiffen the arms a bit and usually eliminate the noise. If you drive in extremely windy locations, it is not unheard of that the wind will override the spring tension and the awning may begin to unfurl. There are aftermarket roller locks that eliminate this potential problem.

198. Some door stays or holders (the hinged piece attached to the outside coach wall used to fasten the door in the open position) tend to flap up and down while driving. This can make a racket. Put a piece of hook-and-loop fastener near the end to hold it down against the coach wall while driving.

Oceanside camping such as Key West offers RVers a great chance to relax and enjoy the ocean breezes.

# Section

*4*

## *All the Other Stuff You Need to Know*

RVing is fun but, as you already know, there is a lot to learn. For example, one "different" type of camping you can do in your RV is boondocking—also called "dry camping." While you may at first think you don't want to be away from the obvious comfort and convenience of your common utilities, most RVs are self-contained. They have everything on board to live comfortably for some period of time with all the conveniences. Being self-contained provides you with enormous freedom and flexibility. Plus, it can significantly lower your costs! It's worth a try.

People who *tow* their RV, a 5th wheel or travel trailer, naturally have their personal vehicle with them when they arrive. People who *drive* their RV, a motorhome of any size, usually tow in order to have a personal vehicle available for their use upon arrival. So, if you drive your RV, there is certainly some other stuff you need to know.

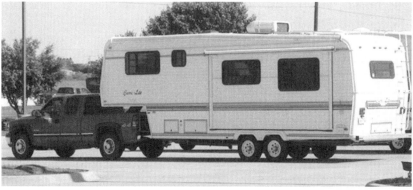
5th wheels are a popular type of RV.

Winter camping is not for the faint-hearted. You must learn those things that allow you to live and play in the colder climates. RVs are built to withstand colder temperatures. From heated compartments to dependable furnaces, many RVers are perfectly content to stay in their RV during the winter months.

Winter camping is popular and available year round.

There are accessories of every description for RVs—from gadgets to necessities. You will need to do your research and make your purchases. What we have detailed in this section are those "major" accessories that can make your RV life safer, more convenient, easier, and hassle-free. Some are expensive. Some are inexpensive. You choose. However, some are absolutely necessary, so think of these as "must haves." Items such as road atlases, campground directories, and jack blocks are necessities. Others are "nice to have," so look and choose carefully.

Last, but not least, is maintenance. Everything must be maintained. Certainly, all those "things" necessary for living comfortably, such as the coach batteries and generator, must be in good operating order. In a drivable RV, that also means engine maintenance. It must be drivable—that is, ready to go and stop—plus, it must be safe. Maintenance is simply a fact of life. You must learn to do it or hire someone to do it. A good compromise is to learn and do what is easy for you and have the rest done at qualified service centers.

Diesel pushers have the engine in the rear. Your maintenance access is here.

# Boondocking (Dry Camping)

## Overview...

The slang term "boondocking" is RVer jargon for "dry camping," that is, camping for one or more nights with no hookups. This

Boondocking is great in the middle of Death Valley National Park and other areas.

means not hooking up to anything. RVs are self-contained. You can carry ample water to survive in comfort for several days and enough LP gas for several weeks in summer conditions. Battery power, while limited, can be conservatively used for many days. If you have an inverter/ charger you can extend the length of time you can boondock. An inverter provides ample 120-volts AC electrical power for operating most appliances for many hours without recharging. To do this you must have a large-capacity coach battery system and limit the use of high-power appliances such as microwave ovens and toasters.

Generators provide recharging capability as well as generating electrical power. Unless you have an inverter/charger with a high charging capacity, the generator will only power the converter on most coaches. This will limit the charging capabilities and result in only partial charging of the battery bank. You will have to decide how long you can boondock by reviewing all your energy requirements and usage.

The generator is mounted outside the coach and is accessible for maintenance.

With holding tanks, all normal, daily functions are readily available. With some unique and easy conservation techniques, RVers often go one or two weeks without having to resupply.

Why would you bother with boondocking when there are plenty of campgrounds around? There are several reasons including...

- **Convenience**... Being able to stop *where* you want and *when* you want is really convenient. Perhaps you are tired after a day's drive and the campground you just called is full. Do you really want to drive another forty miles (sixty-four kilometres) to the next one? Or perhaps you simply do not need to hook up to additional utilities since you just want a night's sleep and plan to get up early and drive. So, why mess with hooking up and unhooking?

- **Cost**... Boondocking is almost always free. As previously mentioned, Wal-Mart, Flying J, Cracker Barrel, and numerous other businesses frequently allow RVers to spend the night in their respective parking lots. There is no cost for this. Occasionally, a full campground in a popular area may have overflow sites available—there are no hookups, so it is definitely boondocking—but they will likely charge a reduced camping fee.

- **Solitude**... Sometimes you just want to be alone and get away from it all. Boondocking is the answer. In the U.S.A., BLM (Bureau of Land Management) lands offer this option as well as other parks and private areas.

---

**Caution**... Do not assume that highway rest areas are totally safe. Some have security patrols. Most do not. Choose carefully and be safe.

---

The biggest problem with boondocking for several days is that your grey water tank fills too rapidly due to water usage. The grey water tank will likely fill 2–4 times faster than the black water.

Follow the appropriate signs when parking. You are no longer just a simple vehicle that can fit anywhere.

Boondocking several days requires that you take on a different way of looking at water conservation. This is not to suggest that you have to live primitively because you don't. Daily showers and cooking meals are a natural part of boondocking.

Many RVers on the road (trying to drive a few days to get to a destination) will often camp one night and boondock for two nights. You can maintain this schedule with virtually no water conservation whatsoever. This will, however, reduce your camping costs by approximately two-thirds, or 66%—a significant savings.

199. Carry a few gallon jugs of drinking water with you. Use these in the kitchen for cooking, filling the coffee pot, refilling drinking bottles, etc. This leaves more water in the water tank for washing, flushing, etc.

200. As the jugs are emptied, carry them with you in your car. When you get to a facility where you can refill these with potable water, do so.

201. If you are a family that uses lots of ice, get an extra bag and put it in the freezer at the beginning of the trip.

202. Purchase condiments that come in a squeeze bottle. Doing this will save using utensils.

203. When you wash dishes, use two containers (like plastic tubs)—one for washing and one for the rinse water. When finished, don't empty these down the sink into the gray water tank. Flush this water down the toilet. Don't forget to turn off your water pump when doing this so you don't waste more water flushing while you dump the dishwater.

   Dump the dishwater only and save the rinse water. Use it as the wash water the next time.

204. Use paper plates, disposable cups, and plastic utensils to eliminate some dishwashing.

205. Plan lots of one-dish meals (casseroles, stews, etc.) to prevent using and washing extra pots and pans.

206. Grill foods outside when possible to eliminate clean up of pots and pans.

207. Use the big plastic bags with seals as mixing bowls.

208. Prepare multiple meals at the same time—to utilize preparation utensils and clean up one time.

209. Use paper towels or the used paper table napkins to wipe excess food from pots and pans prior to washing them. This will save a pre-rinse and may also save running a second load of dishwater.

210. Get a hand-held shower head with a valve that will completely stop the water flow.

211. Never let the water continuously run while brushing your teeth.

212. Limit each person to a half-cup of water for brushing teeth and cleaning their toothbrush and don't run water at all. Pour the half-cup from the water jugs.

213. Use a pan to catch the initial water you must run while waiting for the hot water to come through the faucet. Use this for doing the dishes later. Heat it on the stove or in the microwave.

214. Take the classic "Navy" shower. Rinse quickly—10 seconds or so and shut off the water. Soap and wash as long as you want since there's no water running. Rinse quickly.

215. If the next person showers immediately after the first, you won't have to run the water to pre-heat it.

216. For a quick warm washcloth, wet one, put it on a paper plate, and microwave for about 10 seconds.

217. In some popular boondocking locations (Quartzsite, rallies, etc), there may be services available including both water trucks and the ever-popular "honey wagon" (sewage pumper truck). They will fill your water tanks and pump out your holding tanks—for a fee. Paying this may be more palatable than moving the coach.

    If you have the holding tanks pumped out, be sure you check both holding tank valves after they unhook. Don't want these left open by mistake!

Many RVers spend the night in Wal-Mart parking lots, Flying J Truck stops, Cracker Barrel restaurants, and other businesses. These overnight stays should be just one night's parking, usually arriving in late afternoon or evening and leaving fairly early the next morning. The generosity of these businesses is a wonderful, convenient, and money-saving privilege for many RVers.

Unfortunately, there are those who abuse the privilege by overstaying their welcome, leaving trash scattered around, dumping gray water on the ground, partying under their awnings, etc. Even if the businesses choose to put up with them, there is still a danger of a municipal government passing a "No Overnight Parking" regulation, causing all RVers to lose the privilege—and it is a privilege.

There has been a list passed around various RV groups that establish the "rules" for this boondocking privilege. This list is affectionately known as "Wal-Mart Rules." However, it must be noted that **the list was generated by RVers for RVers and is not officially connected with Wal-Mart** in any way.

## Attention Campers

We welcome you to our parking lot and appreciate your patronage. While you are here, we request that you observe the following rules of courtesy:

- Please limit your stay to one night. Arriving later in the day, and leaving early in the morning would also help us reduce congestion in our parking areas.

- Please empty trash in trash receptacles only.

- Do not empty gray water on the ground or in the sewer drains. If you need to empty your tanks, ask our information desk for the nearest location of an approved dump station

- Please don't extend awnings, set up chairs and tables, or otherwise make our parking lot appear to be a campground. It can result in a loss of privileges.

- Park so that your generator, if used, doesn't bother our customers.

- Park in areas suggested by our staff or near other RVs. These areas are selected for your safety and for minimal inconvenience to our customers and staff.

If you see others violating these guidelines, please let us know.

Thank you!

# *Towing the Toad*

Towing a vehicle behind a motorhome is common and easy to do—with practice. The most obvious advantage is that you have your personal vehicle to use when you arrive at your destination.

The towed vehicle goes by several slang names in the RV industry. Most common is the "toad." Another is the "dinghy." Your dinghy can be towed using three different methods including:

**On a flat-bed trailer...** with all four of the dinghy wheels off the ground. All vehicles can be towed on a trailer. (Observe RV weight limitations)

Towing a vehicle with all four wheels off the ground. You can tow any vehicle in this manner.

**On a two-wheeled dolly**... leaving two dinghy wheels on the ground. Most front-wheel-drive vehicles can be towed on a two-wheeled dolly.

A two-wheeled "dolly" designed for hauling your toad. Either the front or rear wheels of the toad must be mounted on the dolly.

**Four down**... Your dinghy can **possibly** be towed with all four of its wheels on the ground. RVers commonly refer to this last method as "flat towing" or towing "four down."

Common among motorhome owners, flat towing means having all four of the toad wheels on the ground.

To ensure any potential problems caused or enhanced by towing are covered by warranty, some manufacturers test and approve their vehicles for towing behind a motorhome. Towing a vehicle not approved for towing, for long distances, may result in serious damage to the transmission, transaxle/differential, or transfer case. Since the engine is not running during the tow, portions of the drive train may not be properly lubricated.

Do your research to find which brands and models of vehicles can be towed and in what manner. Take a drive through a campground and see which vehicles are being towed. Talk with some RVers, check with RV groups, read magazines, and visit websites for "Dinghy Towing Guides" or similar topics. Entities publishing these guides are typically not manufacturers, so it is the best place to start. Then follow up with the manufacturer's data to ensure towability. It is strongly suggested that you not base the purchase of your toad solely on the word of sales staff. Do your research.

Safety in towing is paramount. Your total vehicle length is increased significantly when a toad is attached to your coach. Additionally, this connection serves as a hinge point allowing each of the respective vehicle's wheels to literally roll in different directions simultaneously during portions of a sharp turn. Your ability to park, even temporarily, is limited due to the increased size of the rig.

The braking ability of the motorhome is decreased with the added weight of the toad literally "pushing" the coach during a stop. Depending on engine size and gearing in the coach, the added weight of the toad may hamper the ability to maintain speed on hills and when passing and decrease initial acceleration. Finally, you must never back up (drive in reverse) with the tow vehicle attached to the coach.

## Tow Bars

Tow bars should be used only on vehicles that have been approved for flat towing—with all four wheels on the ground. Manufacturer's approval will ensure that drive trains won't be damaged during flat towing. Verify manufacturer approval by checking the operator's manual for the vehicle to be towed. There will be specific instructions as to what needs to be done to get the vehicle ready to tow, plus daily distance and speed limitations. Have your vehicle's dealer contact the manufacturer to check for any updates to the operator's manual.

Tow bar design has significantly improved over the years and has all but eliminated the old, rigid "A" frame tow bar using the ball-and-socket connection. Today, most tow bars are flexible, moveable, easy to hook up, and can be attached if the toad is just close to the rear of the coach. One person can actually complete the total hookup but it is still easier with two people.

The toad must have a "base plate" installed under the front. The base plate is attached to the vehicle's frame. Two small "extensions" protrude from under the front of the vehicle. The extensions are the connecting points for each of the two arms of the tow bar.

The tow bar assembly is made up of several parts. Starting from the coach, they are as follows:

**Hitch Receiver**... Usually provided by the RV manufacturer and attached to the RV coach frame, the receiver is a 2-inch (5 cm) square opening that will accommodate one end of the tow bar.

Depending on the height of the toad's attachment points and the height of the receiver on the coach (both heights measured from the ground), you may need a "drop receiver" to reduce the difference to within 4 inches (10.2 cm). The tow bar should be level or rise only slightly toward the motorhome receiver. Drop receivers are available to lower the tow bar in increments of 2 inches (5 cm).

A "drop" receiver is designed to lower the angle of the tow-bar arms. Shown here is a 4-inch (10.2 cm) drop receiver.

**A Safety Issue!** Hitch receivers have capacity ratings determined by the RV maker and the chassis manufacturer. There should be a rating plate on the frame of the hitch receiver showing its rated capacity. If not, contact the RV manufacturer for confirmation of the towing capacity.

You must adhere to the total capacity of the RV (GCWR). For example, you may find that a fully loaded RV can only safely tow about 2,600 pounds (1,179 kilograms) even though the hitch receiver is rated at 3,500 pounds (1,588 kilograms). Ensure that whatever you are towing is under the rated capacity of both the hitch receiver and the towing capacity of your coach. **Be safe!**

**Tow bar**... The most popular tow bars are made up of two flexible arms attached at a swivel point to the part of the hitch that is inserted into the receiver. The hitch end slides into the receiver and is pinned with a substantial steel pin and retention clip. Each tow bar arm is attached to the respective base plate extension on the toad and secured with pins and clips, ensuring a strong and safe connection between the coach and toad.

The adjustable arms of the tow bar allow you to hook up without an exact placement of the vehicle.

When the coach is put in gear and initially rolls forward, the flexible tow-bar arms extend to maximum length and lock into a fixed position for towing. They remain locked in the fully-extended towing position until released by means of a lever (or ring collar) on each arm. Unlocking is required for detaching the tow-bar arms from the toad.

**A Safety Issue!** Tow bars are also rated according to the maximum weight they can tow. After determining your hitch receiver capacity and the weight of your toad, you must buy a tow bar rated above the weight of your toad. It can be rated higher but you will be limited to the capacity of the hitch receiver. Just remember the analogy of a chain made up of links. The chain is only as strong as the weakest link. You do not want to see your toad passing you on the freeway because you ignored the capacity information. **Be Safe!**

---

**Safety cables**… Every state and province requires the use of safety cables (or chains). Most common are the steel cables with a plastic covering and hooks on each end that prevent the toad from veering off should the tow bar connection fail. Safety cables are not part of the tow bar apparatus and are not under tension when towing. Some are coiled for convenience to keep them from dragging on the road. They are only used as a backup system.

The complete tow-bar assembly is shown, ready to tow.

Safety cables can also be attached by being fed under the tow bar, crisscrossed, and then each cable is loosely wrapped around the respective tow-bar arm. Either method will support the tow-bar arms in case of a failure.

Safety cables can also be attached by being fed **under** the tow bar, crisscrossed, and then each cable is **loosely wrapped** around the respective tow-bar arm. Either method will support the tow-bar arms in case of a failure.

When driving over a steep ditch such as coming out of a parking lot into the depression alongside the pavement, the rear of the coach may drag. It is common to damage or even sever the cables when this happens. When a drop receiver is used, the apparatus is closer to the road surface and even more likely to drag. You should inspect your safety cables every time you hook up your toad. Replace them when needed.

A simple drive-by or careful observation of the drag marks left by others is a giant clue that you, too, will likely drag.

**Light Kits and Wiring**... Toad or trailer lights must be connected to the coach lights so that turn signals, brake lights, hazard (warning) lights, and running lights are activated from the coach. Every state and province requires the use of lights on the toad and trailer when towing. Some RVers use magnetized lights that mount on the rear area of the toad. The vast majority of RVers install tow-vehicle wiring and place a permanently mounted receptacle under the front center of the toad. An extension cable (a jumper) plugs into a receptacle on the toad and the coach.

# Tow Dolly

By definition, a tow dolly is a short, two-wheeled trailer, designed for hauling your toad "two wheels up." The tow dolly is designed to accommodate only the front or rear wheels of your toad. That is, one set of your vehicle's wheels is on the trailer, the other set is on the ground. Tow dollies are licensed as a trailer since they can be pulled empty. They are usually unhooked from the coach at the campsite and may be stored up close by pulling the tongue up under the rear of the coach.

Shown here is an empty tow dolly.

If the front wheels of the toad ride on the dolly, then the toad should be wired to the coach so you will have running and brake lights, plus turn signals. If the rear wheels of the toad ride on the dolly, then you must arrange for an extra light bar to be mounted, usually across the hood, for signal lights. The light bar must be wired to the coach. Finally, the dolly must also be wired in case it is pulled empty.

**A Safety Issue!** Before towing on a dolly, confirm that the tow vehicle is suitable for towing in this manner. With the advent of part-time four-wheel drive, there is the possibility of drive train damage even when the normal drive wheels are on the dolly.

Also, newer vehicles have somewhat redesigned steering systems. It is now inadvisable to tow a rear-wheel-drive vehicle with the rear wheels on a dolly because the steering wheels can oscillate uncontrollably at higher speeds. Check with the tow vehicle manufacturer and tow dolly maker before dolly-towing any vehicle. **Be Safe!**

# Supplemental Braking Systems

A supplemental braking system is used to physically apply the brakes of the toad when the brakes are applied in the coach. The purpose is to help stop the overall moving mass of both vehicles—the coach and the toad. As the coach is being stopped, the kinetic energy built up in the toad wants to keep it rolling. When the brakes are applied in the coach, the toad wants to keep rolling. Therefore, the toad actually begins to try to push the coach! A supplemental braking system works in the toad to help slow or prevent it moving forward. Doing so provides a shorter stopping distance for the combination coach and toad.

**A majority of the States and all the Provinces require a supplemental braking system in a towed vehicle.** You have a choice of two basic types of supplemental braking systems. One is permanently installed in the toad and mechanically attached to the tow vehicle's braking system. The other is portable and physically installed only when ready to tow. Both types work well and are widely used. Both types are adjustable and can be set to mimic the driver's braking actions.

The advantage to the installed system is that it is activated by a single toggle switch and it is ready to use. A disadvantage is that it must be installed. Therefore, installation will add to the total cost of the system. It is suggested that a trained installer do this as it may affect the braking system of the vehicle.

The advantages of the portable system are lower costs and the ability to move the system from vehicle to vehicle easily and instantly. However, one might question exactly how many tow vehicles are standing by, ready to tow. The disadvantage is that the system must be unhooked, removed, and stored prior to driving the vehicle—even to just back away from the tow bar after being unhooked—since the apparatus typically consumes the space between the driver's seat and brake pedal.

Both types of supplemental braking systems should come with two "accessories." These include a "breakaway" and "brake system monitor" or an "alert receiver." If you purchase an older supplemental braking system, these may not be available. Most states and provinces require a "breakaway."

The "breakaway" is an emergency system designed to panic-stop the toad should it "break away" from the coach due to a disconnection failure of the tow bar. Safety cables usually prevent the toad from literally taking off as a runaway vehicle. However, a safety-cabled, "loose" toad would crash into the rear of the coach when the coach brakes were applied. An activated "breakaway" causes full panic-stop toad brakes to be applied instantly.

The "breakaway" is a small metal box fastened under the front of the toad and wired or plugged into the supplemental braking system. There is a removable plunger inserted in the breakaway. This plunger is connected directly to the coach by a small cable. In an emergency (tow bar disconnection), the toad would drop back onto the safety cables, they would attempt to extend to their maximum, and the plunger would be jerked out of the breakaway box activating a breakaway system, and commence a panic stop. Granted, it wouldn't be pleasant, but it is the best scenario for saving the toad from a potentially disastrous crash upon separation.

The "brake system monitor" may be as simple as a dash mounted light that tells the driver when the toad brake system has activated and, ideally, that the toad brakes are actually being applied. The brake system monitor may be required to allow the RVer to set the sensitivity of the supplemental braking system. The brake system monitor can be a small receiver that is plugged into a 12-volt socket (cigarette lighter) in the coach.

---

Buying a toad braking system can be a daunting task. There are many competing systems and many ways to achieve the same thing—or so it seems. Every company that sells toad braking systems promotes their strengths and often glosses over their weaknesses. There is no single perfect system that does everything best. However, there are systems that do an excellent job and are convenient to use. Today's RVer is looking for a convenient, proven dependable system. Follow the guidelines below when narrowing down your selection and you will find a system that is best for you. Try not to jump at the first system you look at. You may find that you quickly become dissatisfied with it and may have to spend more money. Talk to other RVers and dealers. Once you understand the various systems, you can make an informed decision and be happy with your choice.

## *Tow Vehicle Braking Systems Overview*

Tow Vehicle Braking Systems are critical since numerous RVers with motorhomes now choose to tow a vehicle. Toads are considered, by law, as a "trailer" in many jurisdictions and therefore, often require a supplemental braking system. There are a number of excellent reasons to consider installing and using a toad braking system The following is a list of some of the reasons and concerns that need to be addressed.

You are strongly advised to check out each item in the list and ensure that you know and understand the risks and requirements associated with towing a vehicle or trailer behind a motorhome.

Here is a list of some of the considerations…

**Chassis and RV manufacturer's requirements**… Most chassis makers provide some guidance such as "The chassis manufacturer recommends the installation of a supplemental brake control system to activate the brakes on the vehicle or trailer when you are towing." This is found in the areas of the RV maker's specification chart referring to the Hitch Rating and Tongue Weight. Typical limits on non-braked trailers are in the 1,000 pounds (454 kilograms) to 1,500 pounds (680 kilograms) range. Basically, all towed vehicles require supplemental brakes.

**Laws of physics**… A toad (under hard braking) can exert up to three times its weight on the coach when the coach is braking. This will exceed most coach braking-system's capabilities.

**State/Provincial laws and regulations**… These laws have often been on the books for many years. However, towing a vehicle behind a motorhome is a relatively recent phenomenon. With this increased usage has come increased awareness that a vehicle being towed behind a coach is no different than a conventional trailer, notwithstanding the fact that it does have a braking system. When the toad is being towed, it is a trailer and it should have a supplemental braking system to comply with the laws.

**Increased law enforcement**… As more coaches tow, along with increased traffic and accidents, law enforcement officials are increasingly giving tickets to motorhome drivers who do not have supplemental braking systems.

**Insurance company requirements**… Various insurance companies have been re-evaluating their risk levels as a result of world events. Many RVers have two separate policies—one to insure their motorhome and the other insuring their cars. These RV policies were originally conceived and first marketed when vehicles were rarely towed. Under some RV policies, when the toad is attached to the coach, it is considered to be covered by the coach policy. This increases the insurer's risk and, upon policy renewal, the insurer often asks the motorhome owner if they are towing a vehicle. If the answer is "yes," they then inquire about the use of a supplemental braking system. In some situations it has been reported that the insurance policy would not be renewed unless a toad braking system was installed.

**Safety and peace of mind**… Last, but certainly not least, safety is often the deciding factor. With increased traffic volume, more road construction and increased delays, road rage and frustration are increasing. Many motorhome owners are seeking to err on the side of caution and have all the help they can get. **With a well-designed and operating toad braking system, the stopping distance for the motorhome and toad combination return to the distance that the RV requires without the toad.** This reduces stress both on the RVer and the RV braking system—and provides an extra margin of safety. With the cost of body repairs today, the cost of a braking system is nominal. No one wants to take a chance with safety when human lives are at risk.

The six types shown in the following table highlight the most common systems available. The "dead" pedal in a toad is attained by turning off the engine and pumping on the brake pedal to bleed off the vacuum in the power brake booster. Once this vacuum is bled off, the power brake is no longer functioning, causing the toad brake systems to require substantially more force (often 50–80 pounds [350–550 kPa] of pressure) to activate the brake.

The advantage of using a system that provides a "live" pedal is that it requires just 10–15 pounds [90–100 kPa] of force to activate. This relieves stress on the brake pedal and firewall of the toad.

| Type of System | Live or Dead Pedal on Toad? | Advantages | Disadvantages |
|---|---|---|---|
| Hydraulic, Surge | Dead | Simple to attach. | No Breakaway. No toad brake monitor in coach. Cables can stretch or bind. |
| Hydraulic, Tied into Coach Braking system | Dead | Requires brake line connection(s). | Brake line connections from coach. No toad brake monitor in coach. |
| Air Pressure–Box Type | Dead | Place on Toad floor. Plug into cigar lighter for power. Easy to transfer to another vehicle. | Most make a brakeaway and a monitor optional. Some use pendulum—systems must compensate for over/under reaction. Must be removed to drive toad. Most monitor system, not toad brake pedal. Cigar lighter may not have power when key off. Cigar lighter plug may bounce out of power source. |
| Air Pressure from Coach | Dead | Low cost. | Coach must have air brakes. Possibility of upsetting coach brake balance. Possible warranty issues on coach. No toad brake monitor in coach. |
| Electric | Dead | Control and monitor in coach. | Somewhat difficult to install. Electric motor and shaft needs to be installed to tow. |

| Type of System | Live or Dead Pedal on Toad? | Advantages | Disadvantages |
|---|---|---|---|
| Vacuum | Live | Power brake operates.<br>Only 10–15 lb. (90–100 kPa) of pressure required to operate toad brake.<br>Coach control and/or monitor of toad brake.<br>Some systems both apply and pull off brake.<br>Newest systems do not need to be removed to drive the toad. | Installation times vary.<br>Some systems have removable box.<br>New toad requires second installation. |

## *Guidelines to Consider and Questions to Ask...*

- Does the system apply the brake—*and pull it off again?*

  - Does it depend on the spring in the power brake booster to return the pedal to the standby position?

- Is there a monitor of the toad braking action in the coach?

  - Is it monitoring the toad brake (i.e., that the brakes are on) or the toad braking system (i.e., that the system operated)?

  - Is the warning for the brake activation visual and/or audible or both?

- Is there a breakaway system?

  - Is it included or optional?

- Does the system come on every time the coach brakes are applied?

  - Can it be adjusted to suit your driving style and toad?

- What activates the system? ...coach brake-light switch, pendulum, G-force controller, pressure of coach stopping on hitch, etc.?

  - Is this system controllable?

  - Can it be overridden or applied manually?

- Can it or does it need to be adjusted to compensate for high-altitude conditions?

- Is there a system test function to ensure operation before towing?

- What company manufactures the system?
  - Where is the manufacturer located?
  - Is this company in any other business?
  - How long have they been making toad braking systems?
  - How long has the system been on the market?
- Is the seller reputable?
  - How long have they been selling these systems?
  - How do I reach them if I have a problem?
- What is the warranty and how long is it in effect?
  - How are warranty repairs handled?
- Is there more than one model for different applications?
- Does the system require installation?
  - Can it be user installed?
  - Are there sufficient and easy-to-understand instructions?
  - Is there a toll-free Help line?
- Does installing the system affect the coach or toad manufacturer's warranty?
- Is it able to be transferred to another toad?
  - If yes, is there a cost and how much?
- Where does the installation take place?
  - In the coach?
  - In the toad?
  - In both?

# Coach and Toad Protection

## *Bras*

Vehicle bras have been available for automobiles for years. These are the black, form-fitted, vinyl covers that are mounted across the front of your personal vehicle. The bras are attached to the toad by using twist fasteners, hooks, snaps, hook-and-loop fasteners, or a combination of these. The bra can remain on the vehicle at all times— whether it is being towed or driven but must be checked frequently to ensure dirt is not accumulating under it.

Bras are used to protect the front of coaches. A more recent development is the use of a clear, tough, plastic film that is custom cut to stick to the front of the coach.

When being towed, bras offer limited protection to the toad from rocks, grit, and other objects tossed out from under the rear end of the coach. A bra provides minimal protection for the front of your toad.

The vinyl bra covers the whole front of the vehicle, typically including the bumper, grill, headlights, and may cover a narrow portion of the front of the hood. They are designed to allow sufficient air into the radiator to sustain engine cooling. If headlights are covered, they use a heavy, clear plastic so your driving lights can be used while the headlight lenses are protected. Bras are also available for your RV.

## Shields

A towing shield covers more of your toad than the bra. Like bras, shields cover from the bumper up but typically also cover the hood, the windshield, and possibly both front fenders of the toad. While shields offer a greater area of protection, they must be removed to drive the vehicle. Shields, like bras, must be custom fitted to your vehicle to offer maximum protection. Custom fitting will also help eliminate the potential for dirt and dust from working in between the shield and surface of the vehicle.

## Rock Guards

A rock guard is an accessory used to prevent rocks (usually kicked up from the rear tires) from flying out from under the rear of your coach. A rock guard is the first line of protection for your toad. The rock guard is usually attached to the RV frame in the rear and hangs down, close to the ground, across the full width of the coach. When you are not towing, the rock guard also provides protection to any vehicle following your coach.

There are four basic types of rock guards. They are the "brush" type, the "solid" type, the "slit" type, and the "mesh" type.

**The brush type**... of rock guard looks like a long brush hanging down from the coach. It is designed so that fast moving rocks, when they hit the brush, will lose their energy and drop.

The brush-type rockguard.

When the coach is moving, air easily moves through the brush so there is no drag. One negative heard about the brush type is that in heavy, wet snow, the brush will become matted with the heavy snow and may become a large frozen lump.

**The solid type**... is a heavy, thick rubber material extending from up, under the coach to near the ground. This type of rock guard simply will not allow any material to pass through. One negative heard about the solid type is that in instances where the air bags are emptied (nearly every time you camp), it may seem to bend under the coach. This will not be detrimental to the rock guard but may appear that way.

The solid rockguard.

**The slit type**... looks solid when the coach is sitting still. The slits are vertically cut to form 4–5-inch wide "ribbons" of the rubber rock-guard material hanging down from the hanger. The slits allow the rock guard to be flexible when air bags are dumped. The ribbons also allow air to pass through when the coach is moving. One negative heard about the slit type is that, like the brush type, heavy, wet snow, will cause the rock guard to become matted when frozen.

The slit-type rockguard in the up position.

The slit-type rockguard when the coach is lowered (air bags dumped).

**The mesh type**… is a plasticized fabric that is stretched between the RV's lower rear bumper area and the toad's front bumper area. It is stretched under the tow bar and cables. It is retained by means of hooks on both vehicles. A stretch-cord system allows the vehicles to turn and flex while providing protection. Stones, rocks, and fine grit are blocked underneath the mesh. The three negative aspects to the mesh type are that (a) it must be installed each time you hook up the toad, (b) if the RV is a diesel with a rear exhaust pipe, you must not allow the mesh to contact the hot exhaust, and (c) if the hitch drags, the fabric will tear, leaving holes that debris can pass through.

Regardless of the type of rock guard you select, consider putting a truck-style mud flap behind each rear dual. These mud flaps are available at reasonable prices from various automotive stores and truck stops.

# Winter Camping

Winter camping is becoming much more popular as younger families take advantage of the RV lifestyle. There are some basics that should be adhered to and there are routines that will need to be adjusted if you want to winter camp. Winter camping is fun—but challenging.

Winter camping is popular and available year round in high altitude and mountain areas.

# Driving Considerations

Road conditions will be dramatically different in snow and ice conditions. The condition known as "black ice" is a reality that must be recognized before safely traveling in winter weather. Black ice is the term used for solid, but clear ice formed on the highway. Because it is clear, the black color of the asphalt shows though the ice—thus the term "black" ice is used. The driver cannot see the ice (it is clear) and he or she may be put in immediate danger, without warning.

Speeds must be reduced. **Exhaust brakes should not be used** (since they could cause an unexpected skid). It is recommended that you leave the toad behind, although some winter campers tow a small trailer for snowmobiles. Braking distances increase and RV tires are not designed to provide the effective traction of snow tires.

Even plowed roads in ski areas and campgrounds may contain hidden obstructions. You must be alert for them. It is best to stay on traveled roads and within the drive portions of campsites. Safe driving in winter conditions require more attention to detail; you should expect and be ready for this. If you have the option, just stay put for a few days!

# Corrosion Considerations

You must acknowledge that road salt, if used on the roads you are traveling, will cause some damage to your RV. Coaches that are undercoated are still vulnerable to the inevitable salt spray that will collect on engine components, body panels, in door locks, around cargo doors and throughout the entire frame, suspension, steering, and brake component areas. It may also penetrate wiring harnesses and cause problems long after the immediate exposure.

# Parking Considerations

218. Choose your place to stop carefully. Ensure it is level so that if the hot tires melt the snow you will still be able to drive out.

219. Always back into a campground site so that you can drive forward when you leave.

220. Park two or three feet (0.5 to 1 m) ahead of where you backed in so that if you need to back up to get moving, you already have a clear track.

221. Watch for overhead obstructions (especially tree branches) since contact with any branches can tear roofing materials—especially in cold weather.

222. If you have access to shore power, remember that power cords—especially the large diameter 50-amp cords—become extremely stiff and inflexible in cold weather.

223. Always use a cord rated for the service amperage to which you will connect (i.e., 30-amp).

224. Check for proper voltage and polarity before plugging in and cover all electrical cord junctions with clear plastic wrap to prevent snow entering the connection.

225. If you are connecting to a water connection, follow the campground's recommendation regarding connections and wrap insulation around the hose.

226. Don't hook up your water hose in freezing weather. Onboard water tanks are heated when the furnace is running, so use the onboard water. Refill your tank as needed from the campground supply. Then disconnect, drain the hose, and stow it.

227. It is possible the campground will ask you to leave the hose tap on to allow a slow trickle of water to flow continuously. This will keep their lines from freezing.

## Camping Considerations

When winter camping, the most common question that RVers ask is "Can I use running water?" the answer is yes—possibly. The following items assume that your coach **has not been winterized**. Therefore, your water and sewage systems are fully functional.

228. Certain outside compartments are automatically heated when your furnace is on. You need to maintain a comfortable level of heat (without your coats on) of about 70°F (21°C) in the main living area of your coach. Doing this will automatically provides sufficient heat to the selected outside compartments where the water pump, water tank, and waste tanks are located. You can also monitor compartment temperatures using a wireless thermometer.

The rule-of-thumb is that there is a temperature differential of 15°F (8°C) between the living and heated storage compartments of the coach.

229. Maintaining this interior temperature **will require** use of the LP-fired furnaces. LP gas is not as efficient at lower temperatures, so consumption will increase.

230. Using other heat sources, such as an electric heater, may help the interior living space, but any exterior compartments that require heat may freeze. Using your coach furnace is mandatory. Using your generator to power an electric heater will not heat the exterior compartments. Using a troublelight inside a compartment will help prevent freezing.

231. When the coach is moved, the wind will force air around the bin door seals and cool down the water tank areas. When you arrive at your destination, make sure your furnace is turned on immediately.

232. Be careful when dumping holding tanks in cold weather. Blade valves can freeze and plastic fittings and handles may become brittle and break.

233. Humidity is a factor that must be controlled in winter camping situations. Just the normal living activity will generate excess humidity that needs to be exhausted through overhead vents.

234. Leave overhead vents open when cooking. Avoid boiling water.

235. If you see water vapor fogging up the windows, open your overhead vents to remove the excess humidity. If ignored, this moisture may penetrate ceiling material and potentially damage roof insulation and support members.

236. If you have slides, be careful when opening and closing them. Overnight snow will collect on the slide awning and must be removed before closing the slide. Removal can be quite difficult because the roof areas will also be snow covered. Use a ladder to gain access and have assistance nearby when working from a ladder in the winter.

You can use your RV after it has been winterized. That is, at a minimum, your water and sewage systems have been drained and contain antifreeze. It is recommended that you winterize the water and plumbing systems before traveling to winter camping areas. Use the RV but leave the water system dry. **The following two items assume that your coach has been winterized.**

237. If you do decide to use your water system, it can be used without the hot water system. However, you must keep the hot water tank on bypass.

---

**Caution**! Ensure that all travelers are aware that they **do not** turn on the hot water tank burner or electric element. If these are turned on without water in the tank, damage will occur to the tank and heating element.

---

238. Carry potable water for domestic purposes. Drink bottled water and use non-toxic plumbing antifreeze to flush the toilet when winter camping.

# Power and Energy Considerations

239. Batteries are the power source for most of your onboard equipment. Batteries lose almost 50% of their power capacity in winter conditions.

240. You must use power conservatively and have batteries in excellent condition to last through a winter night. Discharging a storage battery below 50% of capacity will shorten its life. This is 12.6 volts for most storage batteries.

241. Check the water level in each cell and maintain the proper level for maximum efficiency.

242. If the power drops below 10.5 volts, most refrigerators and furnace control panels will shut down.

243. If you leave a generator running to maintain power, ensure that it is loaded to about one third to one half of its capacity. For a 5,000-watt generator you will probably need to operate two 1,500-watt heaters (on

two separate circuits) to provide the load. Without this load, the generator may run erratically, especially if it is a gas-fueled model, because the spark plugs will carbon up if it is run with little or no load.

244. Ensure that you have more than a half tank of fuel since the generator will draw its fuel from the main tank. The generator is designed to shut down when fuel in the main tank drops below one-quarter full.

245. Make sure you have an operating carbon monoxide detector if you are running a generator.

246. Ensure that any snow is cleared away from the generator exhaust pipe and beneath the generator, since it draws its cooling air from below the coach.

247. Limit your use of the TV, VCR, home theater system, and/or satellite TV receiver to preserve battery power if you are using an inverter.

## Once You Leave Considerations

248. If you are leaving the snow areas and will be traveling in cold, winter conditions, then drain all water tanks (including the water heater) and all water lines.

249. Re-winterize all lines using non-toxic antifreeze and remember to add it to all traps, the toilet, and all holding tanks.

250. Before parking the RV, thoroughly clean off all snow from the undercarriage and pressure wash the exterior and under coach areas to remove road salt and debris. Lubricate jack stands if they were extended while camped.

251. Use the brakes frequently on dry pavement to remove any road spray and salt that may have accumulated on the brake rotors or drum. Removing this spray from the rear of brake rotors requires a definite hard stop to move the calipers and bring the inner brake pads against the rear side of the rotors.

252. Follow the winterization steps from your RV manufacturer, chassis builder, and/or engine manufacturer.

# *Winterization*

If you plan to store your RV and not use it during winter months, you must winterize it. The RV manufacturer, chassis builder, and/or engine manufacturer provides a list of requirements to safely store the RV. Locate these instructions and follow them carefully. Some manufacturers recommend driving a coach at least 10–15 miles (16-24 km) every 4–6 weeks. The goal is to warm up the engine and drive out condensation, lube the transmission and differential, and keep brakes functioning.

The basics include ensuring there is no water left to freeze, providing clean engine oil and filters so that acids from combustion do not attack the lubricated components over the storage period. Fuel tanks and fuel must be protected. Living areas

Camping in the winter creates extra challenges.

must be sealed from the elements, humidity reduced, and provisions made for prevention of infestation from mice, other rodents, birds, and insects.

Most of the following items can be completed by the owner—based on their skill level. If you are unsure of how to accomplish these tasks, you may need to hire someone to have it done. Check with your RV dealer.

## Exterior and Chassis

253. Top off with distilled water and charge all batteries. Remove them, if desired. Store indoors above freezing and away from any sources of ignition or open flames.

254. Clean battery cases and terminals using baking soda to remove corrosion; then, protect with grease or special battery terminal coatings.

255. If you remove battery cables, **properly mark each cable**. Months later, you will not remember which one goes to where when they are all loose!

256. If your annual maintenance include some form of rust inhibitor sprayed on the bottom of the RV, then have this treatment completed before you winterize.

257. Fill the fuel tank(s) and add fuel stabilizer if the RV will not be used for more than 30 days.

258. Ensure the shutoff and safety valves are closed or switched off when filling a propane tank.

259. Check the strength of your antifreeze and its pH with test strips available from your chassis dealer. If the antifreeze is a long-life type, you may be able to extend the change interval to four or

Having the propane tank filled is a normal part of RVing.

five years. Conventional (green) coolants require changing every other year.

260. Top off your windshield washer fluid with premixed windshield antifreeze. Operate the washer system to draw the fresh fluid throughout the total system.

261. Winterize your generator. Change the oil and filter according to the manufacturer's instructions. Let it draw in the stabilized fuel by running for 5–10 minutes. Check the antifreeze strength and

There is always access to check your generator's fluid levels.

condition if it is water-cooled. Change the air filter every other year.

262. Service, or have the chassis serviced by a dealer. Lubricate all chassis zerk (grease) fittings including the hidden ones on the steering gear or shaft, change the engine oil and oil filter, and lubricate the exhaust brake, if applicable. For rigs with air brakes, lube the actuator cams and slack adjusters.

263. Change the fuel filter(s) on all gas rigs at least as frequently as recommended by the chassis manufacturer, but no less than every other year.

264. Change the fuel filter(s) on all gas rigs at least as frequently as recommended by the chassis manufacturer, but no less than every other year.

265. Service the air dryer on a diesel chassis and manually drain the condensate from the air storage tanks after parking in the storage location.

266. Lubricate all slide mechanisms (dry lube), door locks (silicone, graphite, or corrosion blockers), hinges (silicone), and catches (silicone) using the appropriate lubricant as noted in parentheses.

At an RV show, several coaches are on display with their slides out. Note the first trailer has its slide in. All need lubrication.

267. Lubricate your automatic entry step with the recommended lubricant.

268. Protect and lubricate all rubber slide seals and door gaskets (special rubber lubricant or silicone).

269. Clean the awnings and slide toppers according to the manufacturer's instructions. Use the recommended cleaner (if required), dry, and properly store.

270. Check the caulking around windows and body panels. If deteriorating, remove completely and reseal with recommended sealant. Failure to do so on a laminated fiberglass body could lead to serious sidewall delamination requiring serious and expensive repairs.

271. Clean and wax the exterior.

272. Clean the roof. Check for any deterioration of seams, repair, then treat, if required. Clean the air conditioning air filters (inside), lubricate bearings, if required, and check all exterior cooling fins for damage and debris.

273. Check all exterior lights and ensure that all operate correctly.

274. Fully inflate all tires to the maximum air pressure shown on sidewall, or to the pressure recommended by the manufacturer's placard located near the driver's seat and examine the treads for uneven or unusual wear.

275. Lubricate all jack stands with grease if there are zerk fittings, or with silicone spray. Ensure that the hydraulic system is full using the proper fluid (usually automatic transmission fluid—check manufacturer's recommendation).

276. One of the most common "technical" complaints/ questions from RVers is, "Why does my [Appliance] not work?" If you want to extend the life of all electronic circuit board connections (common to appliances), learn the following maintenance item early in the life of an RV and you will likely avoid future problems.

    Carefully remove the exterior cover from the furnace, remove the white circuit board connector and apply a corrosion blocking material and reinstall. Replace the cover. Open the water heater cover and repeat with the board connector on it, as well.

    Most suggestions revolve around cleaning connections, etc. You should learn to do this maintenance or ask your RV dealer to do it and show you how.

277. Cover the refrigerator vent and water heater grill to prevent snow, rain, and critter penetration if the RV is stored outside. Open a garbage bag and place it over the door or vent assembly. Then close the door or re-install the vent cover.

278. If you store your RV in an area where animal or insect infestation is a concern, then cover the furnace vents. However, be careful when using tape since the remnants will be difficult to remove in the spring.

279. Empty all items from the cargo bins that might corrode or absorb moisture.

280. Park the RV tires on wooden surfaces such as plywood, even if parked on concrete or asphalt. Place plastic sheeting over the ground if stored indoors above an earthen floor.

281. If parked outside, it is advisable to park over a hard surface, not grass.

282. Cover the tires with plywood or commercial wheel covers to prevent UV damage to the tire rubber.

283. Deflate all suspension air bags if recommended by the chassis manufacturer and retract all leveling jacks. Spray exposed chrome shafts of jacks with a silicone lubricant.

## Interior and Coach Systems

284. Clean countertops, sinks, and toilet bowls with products designed for RV applications.

285. Drain grey and black water tanks.

286. Remove the plug on the bottom of the hot water tank, open the pressure relief valve, and drain the tank. Use a vacuum cleaner and a special tool called a "tank saving flushing tool" to remove the scale and dirt build up at the bottom of the tank.

287. Drain all water lines and blow out residual water with low-pressure compressed air. Make sure you include exterior showers, toilet, and ice maker lines. Follow refrigerator manufacturer's recommended winterization methods.

288. Remove all water filters and install bypass hoses as required.

289. Place water heater in bypass mode.

290. Use non-toxic plumbing antifreeze in all water lines (if desired). Connect to a fitting near the water pump inlet side and allow it to pump antifreeze through to each tap.

291. Winterize the toilet by holding down the water fill or flushing mechanism until the pink antifreeze flows freely. Be sure to pour some into the black water holding tank. Then pour a couple of inches of antifreeze into the toilet bowl and leave it there.

292. Add non-toxic plumbing antifreeze to each sink trap and plumbing fixture. Pour enough to ensure that a quantity flows through to the grey-water tank.

293. Clean, dust, and vacuum the interior and dry any carpet sections that may have gotten wet.

294. Wash all hard floor surfaces.

295. Ensure that you have removed all foodstuffs—especially canned and bottled goods—that will freeze if left in the RV.

296. Remove all items that will absorb moisture in cupboards or drawers.

297. Remove everything from the refrigerator and freezer, wash out containers, clean shelves, empty any water in the ice-maker tray, then leave all the doors open.

298. Clean the oven, stovetop, and microwave oven.

299. Clean all mirrors, shower stalls, and doors.

300. Open all cabinet doors, drawers, and cupboards on exterior walls so that air can flow through.

301. Leave open all interior doors to promote air movement and reduce the potential for condensation.

302. Close all blinds and curtains for security reasons and to ensure there is less fading of upholstery.

303. Remove any electronic equipment that may not be suitable for winter conditions.

304. Remove all fire extinguishers. Store above freezing.

305. Remove all dry cell batteries from all two-way radios, smoke and CO detectors, TV/VCR/DVD/home theater/CD remote controls, flashlights, alarm clocks, and any other portable equipment to be left unused in the RV. Change smoke and CO detectors annually.

306. Turn off LP gas detector.

307. If possible, leave a roof vent partially open to allow air to flow; however, if the RV is stored outside, ensure that snow or rain will not enter.

308. Turn off all battery disconnects.

309. If you are storing your coach in the winter, use fabric softener sheets to deter mice and other small critters. Scatter the sheets around the coach both inside and in the outside compartments.

# Preparing to Use Your RV After Storage

Preparing your RV for use after a long winter is a more pleasant task. If your RV has been winterized, there are only a few steps necessary to begin to use it again.

## Exterior and Chassis

310. Top off with distilled water and charge all batteries. Reinstall them if removed.

311. Turn on the propane tank shutoff and safety valves.

312. Start up the generator and run it under a load for 1–2 hours. **It is very hard on a generator to run it with little or nothing "loading it"**—that is, drawing a significant power. Gas generators, especially, will carbon up quickly (since they are designed to burn some oil) and will begin to surge and almost die causing the power to spike and dip.

313. Lubricate your automatic entry step with the recommended lubricant.

314. Clean off all black streaks if the RV was stored outside.

315. Check all exterior lights and ensure that all operate correctly.

316. Lubricate all leveling (and conventional trailer) jack stands with silicone spray.

317. Reload all removed items into the cargo bins.

318. Ensure that the converter is not obstructed by cargo. It must have adequate airflow to operate properly.

319. Remove the covering from the refrigerator vent and water heater grills.

320. Remove the material used to cover the furnace vents.

321. Remove the tire covers.

322. Fully inflate all tires to the proper air pressure as determined from the vehicle weighing and the tire manufacturer's load charts.

323. Walk around the RV completely looking for signs of damage or areas requiring attention after the storage.

324. Check the roof for damage or items that may be on the roof.

325. Start the engine and carefully watch all gauges for correct readings as the engine warms up.

326. Ensure that the trailer power connection is clean and spray a corrosion blocking material on the exposed connections. Check the pigtail used between the toad/trailer and the RV/towing vehicle for damage and repair. Carefully examine the connectors and apply corrosion blocking material to these connections, as well.

327. On travel trailers and 5th wheels, check the operation of the breakaway system.

328. Check the electric brakes for correct operation.

329. Lubricate all axles, bearings, and pivot points on suspension according to manufacturer's recommendations.

# Interior and Coach Systems

330. Reinstall any water filters and store the bypass hoses.

331. Reinstall all drainage plugs.

332. Turn the water heater bypass valve to "Normal" or "On."

333. Close all drain valves in the water system.

334. Turn on all battery disconnects.

335. Replace all non-perishable foodstuffs that were removed in the storage process.

336. Close all cabinet doors, drawers, and cupboards on exterior walls, paying close attention to any damage that may have occurred over the period of storage.

337. Open and test all blinds and curtains.

338. Return any electronic equipment that may have been removed and check its operation.

339. Replace all fire extinguishers. Check their gauges or test pins for the proper charge.

340. Reinstall all dry cell batteries that had been removed from all devices.

341. Install new batteries in smoke and CO detectors.

342. Turn on the LP gas detector.

343. Turn on the stovepipe and ensure that the burners give a good blue flame, then turn off.

344. Use the following procedure to sanitize and disinfect the water tank:

- Refill the water tank until it is about a quarter full. Then add $1/4$ cup (60 milliliters) of liquid bleach for every 15 gallons (57 liters) of tank capacity. It is easier to premix the required mixture in a plastic bucket and pour into your water tank inlet. Add another quarter tank of water.

- Turn on the water pump and open each hot- and cold-water tap, including the toilet, to drain the non-toxic plumbing antifreeze. Allow the bleach mixture to flow until the chlorine smell is evident. Let this mixture sit in the water tank and water-heater tank for 30 minutes. Then drive the RV for fifteen minutes to slosh this mixture around in the tanks.

- Drain the water tank completely. Add fresh water and pump it through each tap to remove the bleach from the lines. Drain, flush, and fill again. The tank, water heater, and pipes are now sanitized and ready for the season.

345. Remove all fabric softener sheets used to provide protection against mice and rodents.

346. Turn on the refrigerator, water heater, and all furnaces and ensure they all operate correctly.

347. After turning on the water shut-off valve for the icemaker, allow the icemaker to cycle with the refrigerator operating. Throw out the first batch of ice since it may have some plumbing antifreeze in it.

348. Turn on the RV air-conditioning systems.

349. During the first drive, operate the engine air-conditioning system (dash air) to lubricate the compressor seals.

350. Take the RV for a drive and determine that the brakes, including the exhaust brake, operate without pulling the RV to one side or the other. Listen for unusual sounds and carefully watch all gauges for irregular readings. Fully warm up the RV and satisfy yourself that the storage did not affect its operation or condition. If any unusual situations show up, arrange to have them repaired as needed.

# Accessories, Services, and Extra Stuff

Just like homes and apartments, there are a gazillion gadgets available for your RV. Some are good. Some are useless. These are available through stores, on the web, catalogs, and magazines. However, there are some true accessories that are reliable, helpful, and necessary.

Some RVs are equipped with outdoor entertainment centers. You can sit outside and watch your favorite show.

Since the RV lifestyle is different, and storage space is usually at a premium, you should select both your accessories and gadgets with care. Make sure you need them first. Then, if possible, purchase them with a trial period.

Drive through a campground, talk with other RVers, and join an e-mail group to ask about accessories. Visit a major RV rally to browse exhibit booths offering many of the products. The RV rally will also allow you to talk with other RVers.

What is offered here are accessories that make your RVing safer, more comfortable, easier, and fun. Our list includes both products and services for your RV. This could never be a complete list since some are based on individual preferences. The following items are in no particular order.

## Sun Shades

Window coverings, known generically as sun shades or sun screens, are used to cover your coach windows (usually when parked for a few days). Sun shades will help block sunlight from heating up the coach. This will reduce the time you need to run your air conditioner. They also help block UV rays to

White sun screens attached to a coach.

help prevent or slow down fabric fading and wood from drying out.

Sun shades block the view from the outside. You can see out, but people cannot see inside during the daytime. They can see inside at night and during really dark, overcast days, especially when there is a light on inside the coach. Be sure to close your interior privacy curtains at night.

Sun shades almost always have to be custom made—sometimes on site—from a mesh material sometimes called "solar screen" that is designed for outdoor usage. Two common colors are available—black and a pale beige. Black sun shades seem to provide the best visibility for looking out. There are types of sun shades designed for indoor usage.

Black sun screens attached to a coach.

Sun shades are attached to the coach with snaps, clips, hook-and-loop fasteners, or other devices. Attaching most models of outdoor sunshades may require the use of a ladder.

Some models can be attached without the use of a ladder (i.e., with you standing on the ground) and there are no "snaps" drilled into the coach. This type is held on with industrial-strength suction cups and elastic cords. Another type of sunshade, or sun blocker, is available for inside use. These look like aluminum foil and unfold to cover the windshield. There are similar types for personal vehicles and are prevalent in the south.

A reflective shade is available to mount on the inside of the coach. These require no permanent attachment. You cannot see through the reflective shades.

# Digital Video Recorder (DVR)

As a replacement for the standard VCR (and all those tapes), DVRs are now inexpensive, easy to use, take less room, and are more efficient than VCRs. DVRs are used exclusively with satellite TV reception. You can get a DVR for your coach in two configurations. One is an add-on to your current satellite receiver that is solely a recorder. The other option is one that is actually a satellite receiver with a built-in recording device. The recorder is digital and the least expensive option will record about 35 hours of material (at the lowest quality)—equivalent to about 6 VCR tapes.

When hooking up the recorder the first time, you must be connected to a traditional, landline phone. It downloads the initial information needed to start. You will occasionally need to attach it to a phone line to automatically updated the stored information.

# CB Radio

A CB radio is a handy device for checking on traffic conditions especially when sitting in major congestion, stopped, in a strange city. Some new models of CBs are "self-contained" or all the major components are built into the handset—no more big metal boxes to hide.

One major reason to have a CB is that the newer models contain the emergency weather channels. By simply turning on the unit and selecting the NOAA (National Oceanic and Atmospheric Administration—National Weather Service) channel, your CB **will automatically pick up the local weather conditions**.

Many coaches are pre-wired for CB radios. This is sometimes found in the listing of coach specifications or options and is often listed as "CB ready." Often, the wiring is tucked up under the dash (driver's side), ready to use.

If your coach is not pre-wired or "CB ready" you will need to install a CB antenna and run the cable to the CB location. The antenna should be suitable for marine use or a "no-groundplane" model that is suitable for use on fiberglass bodies such as those found on many RVs. Some RVers find it difficult to mount the antenna on the RV body and have elected to mount it on the rear ladder. After the antenna is installed, it should be tuned to the CB radio. While you can do this yourself, it is often easier and less expensive to have a CB

A CB antenna mounted on the ladder at the rear of a motorhome.

specialist, often located at truck stops, make the adjustment and eliminate the cost of buying the necessary equipment.

# Bike Racks that Allow Towing

Many RVers towing vehicles also want to bring along bicycles. With the improvement in the structural stability of newer RVs, there has been a decline in the number and size of cross vehicle storage bins (storage bins that pass completely through the RV and are accessible from either side). For RVers that were in the habit of storing their bicycles inside,

An example of a towable bike rack allows the RVer to carry 3 or 4 bicycles and tow a toad.

this change has resulted in a need for a simple way to carry bikes. There are bike racks to carry 3–4 bikes on a rack fitted to the hitch receiver that safely allow a toad to be towed.

# Headlight and Signals "ON" Reminders

Almost all toads have some feature that reminds you that your headlights are "on" when you turn off the ignition. Some actually turn the lights off for you. RVers have come to expect this feature in all vehicles. Unfortunately, most self-propelled RVs do not offer this feature. It is available as a simple add-on kit that will reduce the risk of leaving the lights on and draining the battery.

Turn-signal flashers on RVs are often hard to hear and many dash signal indicator lights are hard to see. Inevitably, RVs are driven with the signals on, unknown to the driver. A simple add-on kit provides a warning tone loud enough to be heard over the engine and wind noise in modern RVs.

# Front Side-Mounted Turn Signals

As other large vehicles have become more aerodynamic, the old "lollypop" style of signal lights have disappeared from the front truck fenders. These have been replaced with numerous signal lights visible along the side of trucks and trailers. Busses also have signal lights along their sides.

Fortunately, RV manufacturers have begun to realize the omission of this critical signal light prevalent on larger vehicles. For those without lights there are easy-to-install kits available that are placed near or on the front side RV cap. These lights provide warning to an unsuspecting vehicle driver that the coach is attempting to move into the occupied lane.

# Inverter

Inverters take 12-volt battery power and produce 120-volt AC power. More and more RVs have an option to order a small 300–600 watt inverter sufficient to operate a TV and/or VCR for a couple of hours without operating the generator.

On larger, older (typically diesel-powered) RVs with four or more 6-volt battery banks (connected to provide 12 volts), the RVer can add a larger inverter/charger. This system will provide much more AC power for longer times. Many have a comprehensive charging system to effectively recharge the coach batteries when AC is available from the generator or shore power. All inverters must be installed very close to the coach batteries. You must consider the amount and location of extra weight if adding batteries to supply power for the inverters.

An inverter shown mounted in the electrical compartment of a motorhome. The coiled, shore power electric cable is stored below. Inverters are mounted close to the coach batteries.

# Solar Panels

With the advent of lower cost, powerful inverters, the booming demand for residential style features in RVs, and the desire of many RVers to "boondock," there is increased demand for solar panels to provide passive power to recharge their coach batteries. These panels are rated in watts and larger ones now range between 75 and 120 watts. Usually two or three panels provide sufficient power to recharge the batteries and replace power used. These panels are roof mounted and require a charge controller, but otherwise they are carefree. There are numerous sources for information and the interested RVer should first develop a power needs profile. Then work through the system back to the size of battery bank required and the size and number of solar panels to install.

# Rear-View Monitor System

This feature is standard on many larger self-powered RVs and is a valuable addition to a coach. RV manufacturers may provide for this option by pre-wiring, so installation may be a matter of locating the cables and mounting the camera and monitor.

A rear-view monitor is ideal for viewing directly behind you.

An emerging trend is the addition of one or two small cameras at the front corners of the RV attached just below the mirrors. These cameras provide a view of the adjacent lanes and traffic alongside the total length of the RV.

Other small cameras may be located at the rear bumper area to look at the tires on the toad. Most new RV monitors can accept one or more additional camera inputs and the accessory camera kits include a feature to scroll through the views.

Monitoring systems are also used as security when parked. Some RVs now have a small monitor located in the bedroom, near the head of the bed. If you are wakened by noises, this monitor can provide a view of the surroundings alongside and behind the coach.

## Remote Slide Controls

With the popularity of slide-out rooms in RVs and the increasing number of them, RVers are seeking remote control of these slides so that they can operate them from outside their RV. By being outside, you can monitor your slides

The front slide on this motorhome is shown in the "out" position.

and prevent them from hitting any obstructions. These key-fob sized remotes, control the slides instantly, and can be installed at any time.

## Unusual Road Atlases

The classic large (about the size of a folded newspaper) road atlas is a necessity if you are traveling. There are two "unusual" ones that may be helpful and both contain the normal array of maps.

**Wal-Mart**… sells a road atlas with a listing of their stores, with addresses, in the atlas. If you occasionally boondock at Wal-Mart, you can locate the store. Entering the store's location in your mapping program (or while on the Internet) will provide you with a map and directions.

**Motor Carriers**… road atlas is specifically designed for "Motor Carriers" (truckers). This atlas contains some useful information for all states and provinces including:

- Phone numbers and websites for construction and weather-related road conditions
- Low clearance locations
- Legal size/weight limits for interstate (federal) routes and states/provinces
- Police phone numbers
- Emergency phone numbers
- Area codes.

The Motor Carriers' road atlas is available at truck stops and mapping companies. Check the publication date to get the latest information.

# Mapping Software

Mapping programs are designed to help you define **how to find** and **how to get to** where you want to go. They accomplish this by allowing you to type in a specific address or relative location such as a phone number, ZIP/Postal code, etc. that you want to find. The mapping program will find that location and pinpoint it for you on the actual map.

By adding a second address—your starting location—the mapping program will calculate the actual route you can take. This could be across town or across the country.

Mapping programs are sophisticated, allowing you to designate that you must go through a certain place. For example, if you were planning a trip from Minneapolis to Dallas, the mapping program should find the direct route—Interstate 35, south. However, suppose you wanted to stop in Chicago as part of the trip. You could tell the mapping program to route you through Chicago, and it would automatically create a new route. Many mapping programs are designed to also work with GPS systems.

# GPS (Global Positioning System)

A GPS system keeps track of your location (called coordinates). The GPS receiver and antenna (a small accessory on your dash or a remote roof-mounted antenna) actually receives signals from a number of satellites. Multiple signals are compared and your location on the planet is known and can then be tracked as you move.

GPS systems are becoming more common and therefore, lower priced. With that, many RVers are using them.

You can purchase a stand-alone GPS system that includes the antenna and a small monitor. RVers may find that using GPS software and a mapping program in a laptop computer will be much easier to see.

The mapping program works the same—you must type in where you want to go. Then the mapping program automatically identifies the starting location based on your GPS coordinates and automatically creates a route—from point to point.

Some GPS systems will create a set of directions that can be printed or shown on the laptop screen. These directions will identify every turn, remaining distances, even remaining driving time (based on your speed) for the trip. For those of you who are "directionally challenged," the GPS system and mapping software will be invaluable.

# Camping Organizations and Clubs

There are numerous e-mail groups associated with RV brands—usually called "owner's clubs"—and these are often run by individuals, not manufacturers. These groups provide a forum for discussion usually related to a specific brand and encourage both technical and general questions from users. These are an excellent source of information for the new RVer and costs (if any) are minimal.

Many RVers belong to more than one. The "advantages"—as promoted by the respective organizations—include discount camping, discount purchasing, offering specialty products (emergency road service, insurance, RV loans, etc.), "private" camping, guaranteed camping sites, books, magazines, rallies, caravans, maintenance hints, advice, and just an occasional good-old-fashioned-get-together with other RVers who have something in common with you.

You can spend lots of money to belong to these groups. Many have annual dues that are relatively inexpensive and the monthly publications alone are worth the cost. The most expensive are the "resort" memberships—sometimes costing thousands of dollars.

You must do your research. Check their respective websites. Call the groups and ask for materials and sample publications. Talk with other RVers about the various advantages of belonging. Visit RV trade shows and you may see exhibit booths manned by some of these groups. Again, do your research.

The are numerous e-mail groups associated with RV brands—usually called "owner's clubs"—and these are often run by individuals, not manufacturers. These groups provide a forum for discussion usually related to a specific brand and encourage both technical and general questions from users. These are an excellent source of information for the new RVer and costs (if any) are minimal.

## Rallies and Caravans

An RV rally is a gathering of RVers, usually with something in common. A rally may be carefully organized or simply an informal gathering. Rallies take place year round.

Rallies are a great way to meet other RVers and obtain information about your RV, travel locations, accessories, obtain warranty service, and possibly even out-of-warranty service. In addition, local area tours are often offered as part of the rally and many times pre- or post-rally events are held. Most are offered as part of club membership. Therefore, a rally hosted by some national organization may have thousands of RVs attending. National clubs often have chapters that may be based on geographical locations. Rallies for the chapter meetings are often closer to your home and these rallies may be as small as 5–10 RVs and held over a 2–3 day timeframe. Other rallies are based on the brand name of RVs.

Activities are typically planned at the rallies. These range from potluck meals to crafts to seminars. There is lots of socializing, meeting new people, and usually learning something.

Caravans are organized tours with a "wagon master" (usually a couple that plan and lead the RV tour). You pay for the caravan and travel together to predetermined destinations with other RVers. Some caravans give you a little flexibility in daily travel times; however, most of the events, dinners, and campsites are planned for the group and you need to be at the destination by a certain time.

Some tours use CB-radio communication. All RVs travel together and receive a "traveling" dialogue about the area through which you are driving. If the caravan is scheduled over many days, a "tail gunner" or mobile mechanic will be the last RV and will provide light emergency service if an RV is disabled along the way—or, at least, will know how to get professional help.

Some caravans drive a distance, load onto a river barge or a rail flatcar for a period of time, and then depart a considerable distance away. Check out these exciting ways to see many wonderful destinations through the eyes of an experienced tour guide who just happens to share your interest in RVing.

## Emergency Road Service

Many RVers believe that emergency road service is a "must have" when traveling. Due to the size of many coaches, it may be nearly impossible for you to do something as simple as changing a flat tire. In fact, many coaches do not have spare tires! It would be a stretch to think that even the most ardent RVer would carry tools necessary for fixing a tire. Mostly, when you need road service, you really need service!

Emergency road service is offered by various RV organizations for an annual fee. There are private companies—some associated (loosely or otherwise) with major automobile insurance companies—that offer this service. Another source is through dealerships.

Two types of payment are currently used when the on-site repair or service is completed. One is that you pay the bill to the person who does the work, when the work is completed. You must then submit the paid bill to your emergency road service company for reimbursement. The second type is sometimes called "sign and drive." This means that the emergency road service company has prearranged payment with the company actually doing the service (on site). You have to "sign" indicating that the service was completed and you can "drive" away and continue your trip.

You must do your research. Check respective websites. Call the companies and ask for materials. Talk with other RVers about the various policies. Visit RV trade shows and you will likely see exhibit booths manned by some of these companies. Again, do your research.

## Campground Directories

Generally considered a "must have" when traveling, campground directories are definitely worthwhile. They attempt to list everything about every campground, everywhere! Directories are available at camping supply stores, campgrounds, and clubs.

The most common feature RVers use on the road is the phone numbers. While traveling, you can usually determine, within a few hours, where you are likely to stay that evening. Using the directory, find a campground in that general area and call for reservations. In peak travel areas and seasons, you do need to call if you want hookups!

The next important feature is the directions to the campground. While the companies publishing the directories attempt to be accurate, when you call, ask the campground to verify the directions.

Make your own list of questions to ask. You want the campground to fit you. For example, do you want to unhook the toad and back into a site—just for a few hours sleep—or do you want a pull-through site? Do they offer any discounts? Do you need their laundry? If so, how many washers and dryers to they have? Are they all working?

Campground directories are also available on CD. Using the directory on your computer provides a means to search for various types of information.

## Jack Blocks

Using your jacks when parked will support and stabilize your coach. Do not use your jacks for temporary parking (even overnight) when boondocking at courtesy businesses such as Wal-Mart and Cracker Barrel. However, using your jacks at campgrounds is fine.

Unless there is concrete or tightly packed aggregate under your jacks, you will need something between the bottom of the jack and the ground. Otherwise, your jack will simply sink into the ground. Sometimes this happens rapidly, when you are first setting up the coach. Sometimes this happens slowly, and you wake up in the middle of the night wondering why the coach is leaning.

You can purchase or make jack blocks. Camping supply stores sell a tough, composite material made into square, flat blocks. These stack for additional height. Check the package to find the weight maximum for these blocks. Some blocks are designed for smaller, lighter-weight coaches.

For a lower cost option, visit your lumberyard and purchase a **pressure-treated**, 2 x 6-inch (5 x 15 cm) board. Some RVers also use larger boards including 2 x 8-inch (5 x 20.3 cm) and 2 x 10-inch (5 x 25.4 cm) sizes. The length you need is based on the number of jacks you have. If you have three jacks, buy a 6-foot (1.83 m) board. If you have four jacks, buy an 8-foot (2.44 m) board. Have the lumberyard cut your board into 1-foot (30.48 cm) lengths. You will end up with two boards per jack and rarely will you need to use them all at once.

Sometimes the ground is so soft that the jack blocks will also push into the ground. If so, try two boards, placed on each other at a 90° angle. Doing this provides a larger surface area in contact with the ground. Finally, if your jack "dug a hole" by immediately sinking, toss a large rock or a few bricks into the hole to help stabilize the jack and prevent additional sinking.

# *Maintenance*

## Engine RV Maintenance and Care

Do not skimp on the recommended lubricants or parts. Follow the manufacturer's methods of maintenance. Too many examples of premature component failure can be traced back to improper maintenance or the use of incorrect lubricants or parts.

This presents some unusual requirements for the RV owner. The last thing you want is to spend time in a repair shop while on vacation. This can be even more important for fulltimers who lives in their RVs. Routine and regular planned maintenance is necessary to prevent (or reduce) roadside emergencies or unplanned trips to the service shop.

Do not attempt to undertake any service work on your RV that you are not fully capable of doing.

A few hints will go a long way to providing RVers with enjoyable and dependable RVs.

351. At the first indication of a problem, deal with it. For example, a sticking step can be corrected within a short time by lubricating it. If the step fails to deploy as someone is leaving the RV, a severe fall with potential injury could result.

352. Read the owners manuals for your RV and its accessories. Establish a maintenance chart specific to your rig based on your usage.

353. Do not skimp on the recommended lubricants or parts. Follow the manufacturer's methods of maintenance. Too many examples of premature component failure can be traced back to improper maintenance or the use of incorrect lubricants or parts.

354. Make safety your priority in service decisions.

355. Preventive maintenance may seem expensive. However, roadside service, inconvenience, and cancelled vacation plans are much more expensive and frustrating.

Included in this section are a number of suggestions that may exceed your capabilities, expertise, and perhaps interest. We have included many general items that anyone (without any tools) should do—such as checking engine oil and battery water. We have included items that are a bit more technical for the owner who is willing to learn and do more in order to save money and certainly extend the life of their RV. Finally, we have included items that will exceed most "at-home" capabilities. These were included so that the serious and frugal owner can discuss this level of maintenance with appropriate service technicians.

---

**Caution**... Many of the systems on modern RVs include computer and other control systems that may be damaged by untrained individuals probing with test lights and unsophisticated test equipment. Check with an appropriate service center before proceeding.

## Chassis Maintenance

356. When parking for more than a few days, top off your coach fuel tank first. This will eliminate the buildup of water (condensation) in your fuel tank.

357. Check the engine oil level daily when traveling and look underneath for telltale drips indicating a potential problem. For many diesel engines, the dipstick may be very long (6 feet/1.8 m!).

358. Check your radiator fluid level, strength, and pH levels. Change it at the recommended intervals.

359. Check the power steering or hydraulic fluid reservoir level and maintain the proper level.

360. Lubricate all chassis zerk (grease) fittings with the recommended lubricating grease. Check the manufacturer's information to find "hidden" grease fittings or visit a dealer and ask the service technician to show you. On the Ford F53 chassis, there is a hidden fitting on top of the steering gearbox, which cannot be seen. It can be located by feeling the top of the steering gear. On many Freightliner chassis, there is a fitting under the rubber boot at the bottom of the steering shaft inside the coach at the floor. Carefully feel for this fitting, cut a small access hole and apply grease into the fitting. Even if you take your coach to a dealer for this work, tell them about these hard-to-find grease fittings—in case they are unaware.

361. Check the hydraulic brake fluid level on non-air brake RVs. If it has not been changed within the last two years, have it changed. Brake fluid is hygroscopic (it absorbs water). If the fluid contains water, it will begin to boil during hard braking and this may show up as brake fade or lack of braking action. Use Ford Heavy Duty brake fluid in whatever brand of gas chassis you have since it has the highest boiling point of any widely available brand.

362. Lubricate the brake caliper slide pins, using the recommended lubricant. If your chassis has these slide pins, follow the chassis manufacturer's maintenance schedule.

This service is imperative to extend the brake life of the chassis and provide safe brake operation. While it is not as likely that an owner would undertake this service, it is unsafe and expensive if this maintenance is ignored or not carried out frequently enough.

363. Check your transmission fluid level when it is warm using the dipstick or on Allison electronic transmissions—use the appropriate method of pressing console shift buttons and noting the results on the digital readout. Change the fluid according to the manufacturer's recommendations and top off with the approved fluid.

## Body and Coach Exterior Maintenance

364. Clean the bugs and road grime off the front of your RV as soon as possible after stopping so that the acids in the bugs do not eat into the finish. Your RV will look better—plus the use of a good quality wax and protectant will provide increased shine and reduced effort in removing these bugs and grime in the future.

365. Lubricate your automatic entry step every thirty days using the recommended lubricant. Remember to lubricate the hidden upper pivot rod bearings in addition to the step links.

366. Lubricate the slide gear or hydraulic mechanisms with the appropriate lubricant. If it is a gear-operated design, then use a dry lubricant, which will spray on "wet" then dry and leave a suitable lubricant with no dust-attracting residue. If the slide contains a hydraulic ram then spray the shiny cylinder with a high-quality silicone lubricant.

367. Protect and lubricate slide seals and cargo bin rubber gaskets with a specific slide seal lubricant or a high-quality silicone spray. Follow manufacturer's recommendations.

368. RV awnings often are pretreated to resist dirt penetration through the cloth fabric. Generally, these should not be scrubbed or you will damage the treated surface. Rinse off any dirt to prevent staining and always store dry. If it is rolled up wet, put it back out as soon as possible afterwards. Vinyl awnings can be washed and scrubbed. They can be cleaned and treated with an awning cleaner and protector.

369. Lubricate all hinges and door locks with a spray silicone or corrosion blocker.

370. Turn off the electricity to the refrigerator before cleaning the rear area. Unplug the AC in the rear vent area. Remove the refrigerator exterior vent and then, remove the metal shield around the gas burner by the metal chimney. Use a vacuum cleaner to remove any rust flakes that drop from the chimney onto the burner. Use a drinking straw to blow any rust flakes from the burner. Before re-assembling, turn on the refrigerator and set it to run on LP. Observe that it sparks and ignites with a light blue flame. If it is

okay, turn off the refrigerator and re-assemble it. Plug in the AC power cord as well.

371. Lubricate all hydraulic jack stands regularly with silicone spray.

372. Each year, apply a suitable lubricant to the TV and satellite antenna gear mechanisms.

373. Check all roof caulking for deterioration and use the proper replacement sealer to replace the removed material. This is especially important if the RV has a rubber roof.

## Interior Maintenance

374. Test all CO, smoke, and LP gas detectors weekly to ensure that they are operating correctly.

375. Test all ground fault circuit interrupter (GFCI) receptacles to ensure they operate correctly. While you are at it, determine which interior and exterior receptacles they protect.

376. If you have a built-in inverter, determine which receptacles have power when the inverter is "On" with the shore power disconnected and the generator off.

377. Locate the circuit breakers that control each 120-volt circuit and ensure that you have a chart of outlets that they control.

378. Locate all 12-volt fuse panels. There will be one for the coach interior systems and two or three for the chassis and other coach systems. Look at the charts or read the owner's manuals so that you know where to look for a blown fuse in the future.

379. Determine which window is an emergency exit (look for red hardware) and ensure that everyone knows how to properly use it in an emergency.

380. Check the refrigerator door seals by closing the door on a currency note. It should present noticeable resistance as the note is pulled out. If not, either adjust the door gasket or replace it.

381. Check the refrigerator door for noticeable and unequal gaps between the upper and lower hinge brackets. With certain brands of refrigerator, it is normal for some settling of the doors. They ship with extra spacers on the top door pin. As the door settles a bit, spacers may be taken from the top pin and inserted under the lower one to raise the door back into the correct position. If there is an insufficient number, then remove the door and add a few similar-sized washers.

382. Use a refrigerator thermometer to confirm the correct adjustment of the temperature controls.

A thermometer that ensures that the refrigerator is cool enough to protect the freshness of food.

383. Check the stovetop burners for a proper blue flame. If equipped with a spark lighter, ensure that it lights each burner quickly.

384. Clean all plastic sinks only with a gentle sink cleaner that is safe for RV sinks and plumbing systems.

# Generator

Generators pump fuel from the main vehicle tank and are designed to automatically shut off when your fuel level is somewhere between $1/4$ and $1/2$ full. The purpose of this is to ensure that your generator will not use all the fuel in the common tank and leave you without sufficient fuel for your vehicle engine.

To find this approximate shutoff point, as you are driving and the fuel gauge drops below 1/2, have the copilot periodically start the generator and run it 2–3 minutes—try this about every 15 minutes of driving. Note where the fuel gauge needle is each time the generator is started. At some point, the generator will start but stall shortly afterward—note that needle position, too. This will give you a rough indication, on your engine fuel gauge, of where your generator can no longer be used. You may want to make a small mark on your fuel gauge for future reference.

385. Check generator oil and coolant levels frequently.

386. Generators need a regular oil change and new oil filter just like your vehicle engine. Either learn to do this,

There is almost always convenient access to check your generator's fluid levels.

(it is easy but sometimes a bit messy) or plan to have it done. Check your operator manual for the frequency required for this maintenance. Generally, it is based on hours of operation or once a year. Also, routinely check and change the air filter.

387. Run the generator **under load** periodically whether you need it or not—check your manual for how much is needed. If there is no recommendation then run it for two hours every thirty days.

388. When recharging your coach batteries by using your generator, run it about 2–3 hours to fully charge them if your RV has an inverter/charger or a newer type converter with a battery maintenance feature.

389. When you are boondocking and parked close to other coaches (such as at a rally), you will need an extension on your generator exhaust pipe. This will prevent exhaust fumes from entering the windows of coaches parked close to you (and yours—if you have the windows open). These can be purchased, but a simple one can be made using PVC pipe. Do not let the PVC pipe touch the hot exhaust pipe.

# Checking Tires

It used to be sufficient to use a small hammer or bat to check the tires. A good bounce indicated that it had sufficient air pressure. Today's RV loads are such that you must regularly use a proper tire pressure gauge to determine the correct tire pressure. Low air pressure will lead to serious and dangerous tire failures and collisions.

If no other guidelines are available, use the maximum tire pressure shown on the sidewall of the tire. Ideally, have the loaded RV weighed and then use the tire manufacturer's tire pressure/load charts to determine the proper air pressure.

390. Using an "air chuck" may be easier to fill tires with air. The "chuck" looks like the standard fill nozzle attached to the end of the air hose. However, when the chuck is pushed onto the tire valve, it "locks" on and you do not have to hold it in place. You may have seen these in use at tire companies. They are very common.

391. Find and record the tire date codes. Tires have a DOT code molded into the sidewall that includes the date of manufacture. To find the date, look for the letters "DOT" and then read the numbers. This code may be on either side of the tires due to the way the tires are mounted and could be between the inner dual tires.

This date is important since RV tires continue to age when not being used. It is recommended that RV tires be changed between five and seven years from the date of manufacture no matter how much tread is left. The date coding on tires made since 2000 has a four-digit date showing the week and year of manufacture. (For example, 0702 means the **seventh** week of 2002) Prior to 2000, the date code contained three digits and a small triangle with the week and last digit of the year (for example, 398 means the thirty-ninth week of 1998).

392. Check the wear pattern of the tread on each tire and, if uneven, have the RV alignment checked. Rotate the tires as required. Most tire makers no longer recommend dual tire rotation unless there is evidence of uneven wear.

393. If any tire is driven with low air pressure, it is best to replace it. The interior damage caused by this condition may not be readily visible; however, it is more likely to blowout. If you have a spare tire, replace the spare with this tire. Otherwise, buy a new tire and keep the potentially damaged tire as a spare.

# Checking Batteries

394. Check your batteries' "water" level and ideally use a temperature compensating hydrometer to check the state of charge. Both the engine and coach batteries are critically important as they affect your living conditions, as well as your ability to drive the RV.

395. Battery compartments are open to the road and a layer of dust and dirt will form on the tops of the batteries. If this dirt layer becomes moist, it can actually discharge the battery. You must keep your

batteries clean. You can safely hose off the dust and debris occasionally. Keep corrosion under control by cleaning the terminals and coating the connections with a corrosion stopping spray.

396. Adding distilled water, multiple times, will cause some spillage and some of the acidic liquid in the battery will end up on top of the battery. Use a spray cleaner (available at auto supply stores) to clean the batteries. Some of the sprays instantly make foam (looks like shaving cream) that will change color if acid is detected. Follow the directions on the can. Generally, you hose off the batteries. Try a second application if acid shows up. Do not do this in your campsite.

397. Some coaches have the batteries located where it is difficult (or maybe impossible) to look into the battery fill to determine how much water is there. If yours is like this, purchase a "battery filler," available from many automotive-parts stores. This pitcher-like container holds the distilled water and it is sealed so water will not spill. There is a spout set at a right angle to the container. By inserting the spout into the battery fill and pushing, a one-way valve opens and allows water to enter the battery.

The good news is that it fills to the appropriate level automatically and shuts off. Plus, the container will help you prevent water from spilling onto the tops of the batteries.

398. Use an old turkey baster for filling accessible batteries. Buy one at a yard sale.

399. Most gas-powered RVs have a converter that converts 120-volt AC power to 12-volt DC power and supplies this to power the coach systems. Most will

also provide power to recharge the coach batteries. However, they will not charge the batteries much more than about 85% of full charge. Some converter makers offer an accessory module that will allow two- or three-stage battery charging, and some even provide trickle charging to the chassis batteries. This addition, if available, will extend the life of your batteries by completely charging them.

The vehicle alternator, a high-capacity, three-stage battery charger powered by the generator, or shore power will fully charge all the batteries. Charging is always necessary when boondocking (dry camping—no hookups) since you are running everything electrical from the battery power in your coach batteries (not engine batteries). If the RV has an inverter/charger, then the generator will provide the power to fully charge and de-sulfate the coach batteries. The generator will charge the chassis battery with a controller (that may be optional), as well.

# 5 Section

## *Border Crossing Stuff*

As you plan your RVing adventures, you will probably plan a trip that will require a border crossing into another country. For those traveling to Alaska, you will definitely have at least one international border to cross. This can be intimidating because it is a new experience.

When crossing a border into another country, you must understand that the rules that apply at home do not always apply in the country you are visiting. You must be prepared for this.

It is impossible to cover all the details necessary since daily events affect what items are important and required by border officials. You should consult with the Immigration and Customs officials in the countries you plan to enter as well as your own country since you will be limited in what you can bring back. Sometimes the limitations are based on the length of time spent out of your country.

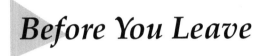

# *Before You Leave*

Have at least two pieces of **photo identification**. A driver's license and health card is usually sufficient if you are a Canadian traveling to the U.S.A. If you are an immigrant, you will need a passport and possibly a birth certificate. You may not normally carry these documents with you. Plan for the time to obtain them if you do not have them in your possession. Ensure that you allow sufficient time for processing by the various government authorities.

Check with your **health insurance** carrier to ensure that you have sufficient coverage in the foreign country. Each country has a procedure for providing health care and you need to understand the system in the host country and how payments are made. Your insurance carrier can explain the procedures. You will be able to purchase insurance with coverage for specific times and limitations. Understand what is covered by these policies, how long you are covered, and the procedure for coverage. Some require payment for services and you submit receipts for reimbursement. Have sufficient credit card limits to handle the unexpected. Some "high-end" credit cards will provide limited out-of-country health insurance as a card benefit. If your trip is under thirty days, this may be the way to go.

Insurance coverage and **proof of insurance** may vary with the country you are visiting. In Mexico, you will be required to buy special insurance immediately upon entry into the country. Generally, throughout the remainder of North America, your insurance carrier can provide coverage for your trip. Obtain the form and keep it in the vehicle. Many states and provinces require that proof of insurance be present in the vehicle. Hefty fines are imposed on those who do not comply. You must understand the process for paying a claim if one occurs outside your country.

If you require **prescription drugs**, ensure that you have a sufficient supply before you leave and confirm with your pharmacy that you can take these drugs, without restriction, into your destination country. Always carry the original prescription bottles for all medications.

You should obtain some **foreign currency** for the country you will be visiting. Canada and Mexico are more willing to accept the U.S. dollar than the U.S. is to accept the Canadian or Mexican currencies. Knowing the exchange rate before you leave your home country can make currency conversion less of a challenge. Your bank can give you the exchange rate. The "official exchange rate" is used by the country's federal bank for buying and selling their currency and you will be charged a premium of three to five percent by the local bank for the exchange. It will cost you more than the actual exchange rate. Some U.S. banks require up to one week to be able to supply you with foreign currency. Canadian banks are usually able to supply U.S. currency. You may need to order Mexican currency.

Border tolls can usually be paid in both currencies. Major **credit cards** are accepted in most large stores and fuel stations. Some cards may not be accepted outside the U.S. (you must verify that your card will be accepted). Make sure you have appropriate limits on the cards and do not carry all your cards in the same wallet or purse. If you misplace that wallet or purse, you will be stranded.

If you have a **pet**, obtain a current certification from your vet that the animal has been immunized within the last year. Dogs and cats do not usually present difficulties as long as you have the papers. Birds and other pets may need to be inspected by a local veterinarian before being allowed into the country. Ask your vet and do your research.

Know the requirements of the country you are entering regarding what you can and cannot bring with you. For instance, it is not legal to bring a weapon for personal protection into Canada. If you are an American entering Canada, you will most likely be asked whether you have a gun. Answer truthfully. However, many before have not been as honest and forthright. Canadian officials may request that you undergo a search. To ensure a trouble-free entry, leave your personal protection weapon in the U.S.A. Canada may allow certain sport and hunting weapons to enter with prior approval.

There are restrictions on bringing in alcoholic beverages and tobacco products. For example, you may be limited to one carton of cigarettes and two, 26-ounce (769-mL) containers of alcohol. Check with the officials in the country before you enter.

Fruits and vegetables—especially citrus fruits—are often restricted. Plan to buy these items in the destination country.

Firewood is restricted across borders. You may be able to bring wood that has no bark on it.

# Preparing to Cross the Border

You may want to refuel your RV, toad, or towing vehicle just before crossing. Fuel costs will vary depending on the federal and local taxes. Generally speaking, fuel is less expensive in the U.S.A. than in Canada or Mexico. While fuel is sold in U.S. gallons (3.79 liters) in the U.S.A., it is sold in liters in the remainder of North America. This can be quite unsettling for the uninformed the first time you re-fuel in the foreign country.

For relatively new (especially expensive) items—such as a camera—you should declare that you are leaving your country with it. For example, when leaving the U.S.A., you can fill out a form stating you have these items with you upon departure. This same form, in turn, allows you to return home with these items without having to prove where you purchased them and possibly pay duty on them.

As you approach a border crossing, pay close attention to which lanes are accessible for RVs. You are never considered a truck—avoid truck lanes. Larger crossings will have a lane designated for RVs or "Cars with Trailers." Watch for signs directing you to special lanes that are wider. You never want to enter a lane to discover you cannot drive through and have to back up. This may be impossible without effort and cooperation—and if you are towing a toad, you will have to disconnect. The distance between booths is just slightly larger than the width of an RV. Drive straight and carefully.

Have all passengers move forward (in a motorhome) and have everyone ready with their proof of citizenship. Take off all sunglasses. As you approach the booth, open your driver's window and push forward the screen so that the official can make direct eye contact.

Answer all questions succinctly **without** adding additional information unless requested. The officials need to ensure they know who is entering their country, how long you are staying, the purpose of your trip, what you are bringing in, and what you might be leaving behind. They will be seeking most of this information by means of a question and answer session. Offering extra details often creates problems. Keep answers truthful and short, be polite and understand these people are doing a very important job.

If officials request to come on board for a more thorough inspection, then you will be given a form and asked to exit the booth area to an inspection station. You may accompany the official on the inspection although they may ask you to leave. The RV is considered your home. If you have concerns about leaving the RV while they inspect, you may request to be present during your inspection. If you are turned down, ask to speak with a supervisor. Be polite in all interactions with the border crossing officials.

# Once You are in the Foreign Country

Take advantage of the state or provincial welcome center. You can obtain the latest information about the area, ask questions, and clarify items that came up in your trip planning. These centers are well organized and larger ones have staff on site during the day to answer questions.

You are the tourist and the rules will be different. Speed limits are shown in different ways. In Canada and Mexico speed is measured in kilometres per hour. One hundred kilometres per hour (100 kph) is equivalent to sixty-two miles per hour (62 mph). All speeds follow these ratios, so you can calculate the conversion by multiplying the miles per hour speed by 1.6 or the kilometers per hour by $^5/_8$.

Most speedometers on vehicles built in the last ten years have both scales, one showing the mph and the other showing the kph. Simply remember that on the highway it takes an hour to go sixty miles or one hundred kilometers. You may have a button to change your odometer to read in kilometers. Doing this is helpful in estimating distances.

Fuel is sold in Canada and Mexico in litres. In the U.S.A., fuel is sold in U.S. gallons, which is 3.79 litres and smaller than the Canadian Imperial gallon which is 4.4 litres. If you calculate fuel economy, you will want to remember the differences and enter them in your calculations.

Many states and provinces require seatbelts to be worn by all occupants of a vehicle and this does include motorhomes. If you have not worn yours for a while, you might want to get them out from under the sofa or dinette if you have passengers in those areas.

Many states and provinces prohibit the use of radar detectors. Their enforcement officials have equipment capable of detecting the use of these devices. If you have one, turn it off. This information is usually posted shortly after you enter the state or province.

Save all receipts for purchases. You may be eligible for a rebate on local taxes. You may also need to verify what you actually purchased in the host country.

The laws in your country may not apply in the foreign country you are visiting. You are a guest—a visitor—and do not have the same rights as the natives. The people may speak the same language but live under a different set of standards. Do not assume that what you do at home is what they do here. Ask, if you are uncertain, and observe before you act. As an example, in many Canadian provinces alcohol and beer is not available at grocery stores. There are special "liquor" or "beer" stores. Conversely in many U.S. states, it is not unusual to see aisles of wine, liquor, and beer in the grocery stores.

Over-the-counter drugs that are unrestricted at home may require a prescription in the country you are visiting. These differences are sometimes quite subtle but they do make traveling a little more of an adventure.

You may also need to be more aware of your circumstances in the foreign country. Maintain awareness of those around you and learn from those you visit as you travel through the area. Many U.S. citizens are surprised to learn that few Canadians carry or have the need to carry personal protection items such as handguns. Many Canadians are surprised to see the high visibility of weapons for sale in local stores in the U.S.A. Each country has different laws and it takes some adjusting to understand and accept these differences.

# Re-entering Your Country

When you are preparing to drive back home, have all your receipts for purchases of the goods you are bringing back across the border to your home. This does not include consumables such as food or fuel.

If you are a U.S. citizen leaving Canada for the U.S., you are entitled to claim back the Goods and Services Tax (GST) paid on any item you purchased that you are exporting. This does not include meals, fuel, or food. If you do not apply when you leave, then you can contact the Canadian Customs and Revenue Agency to obtain the form and submit it by mail.

There is usually a Duty Free store at the border crossing and you may purchase items at this store "Duty Free." They can also process your GST refund.

Be prepared for the same procedure for re-entering your country. Be in the correct lane, have the appropriate documents, and be prepared for questions about how long you were out of the country, what the purpose of the trip was, what was the total value of goods purchased. (Always total it to the penny and have receipts visible.) They will usually ask about alcoholic beverages, cigarettes, and may ask about fruits or vegetables. They may have a "question of the week" which no one is prepared for. Answer politely and directly without additional information.

Once you are across the border and arrive in your home country, you will have a different view of your country and a sense of comfort. There is a sense of security in coming back home and knowing all the rules that apply.

It is a great experience to travel in a foreign country—to see the sights and sounds of it. Once you have traveled throughout North America by RV, you may start dreaming about that trip to Europe, Australia, or other exotic destinations—all of which can be explored by RV.

To explore with a sense of adventure, to live the experiences you had only dreamed of, to meet new people, and to enjoy it all, is the RVing lifestyle. We hope you enjoy the RVing lifestyle and that this book has given you a sense of and desire to explore the fun and savor the experiences that RVing provides.

# Index

# CANADIAN
## ORDERS

### CALL

## 877•266•5398

### ORDER ON-LINE

## www.rv-partsplus.com

### SEMINARS/SPEAKERS

**Contact the author direct at...**
**bob@rv-partsplus.com**

---

# UNITED STATES
## ORDERS

### CALL

## 800•262•3060

### ORDER ON-LINE

## www.rvstuff.org

### SEMINARS/SPEAKERS

**Contact the author direct at...**
**info@rvstuff.org**